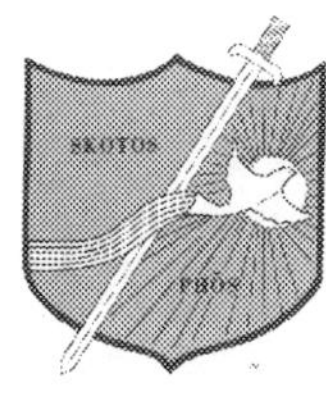

Counseling with God's Word

From A to W

Ovit G. Pursley Sr.

Order this book online at www.trafford.com
or email orders@trafford.com

Most Trafford titles are also available at major online book retailers.

Unless otherwise indicated, all Scripture quotations in this
Volume is from the King James Version of the Bible.

First Edition
First Printing 2010

Ovit G. Pursley Ministries™
P.O. Box 31574
Knoxville, TN 37930

Printed in the United States of America.

ISBN: 978-1-4269-5015-5 (sc)
ISBN: 978-1-4269-5014-8 (e)

Trafford rev. 06/05/2012

www.trafford.com
North America & international
toll-free: 1 888 232 4444 (USA & Canada)
phone: 250 383 6864 • fax: 812 355 4082

Contents

Counseling with God's Word

A-W: Quick Reference

Marriage

Genesis 2:18-25
And the LORD God said, It is not good that the man should be alone; I will make him an help meet for him. 19 And out of the ground the LORD God formed every beast of the field, and every fowl of the air; and brought them unto Adam to see what he would call them: and whatsoever Adam called every living creature, that was the name thereof. 20 And Adam gave names to all cattle, and to the fowl of the air, and to every beast of the field; but for Adam there was not found an help meet for him. 21 And the LORD God caused a deep sleep to fall upon Adam, and he slept: and he took one of his ribs, and closed up the flesh instead thereof; 22 And the rib, which the LORD God had taken from man, made he a woman, and brought her unto the man.23 And Adam said, This is now bone of my bones, and flesh of my flesh: she shall be called Woman, because she was taken out of Man. 24 Therefore shall a man leave his father and his mother, and shall cleave unto his wife: and they shall be one flesh. 25 And they were both naked, the man and his wife, and were not ashamed.

Genesis 2:18, 24
And the LORD God said, It is not good that the man should be alone; I will make him an help meet for him. "...Therefore shall a man leave his father and his mother, and shall cleave unto his wife: and they shall be one flesh."

Ephesians 5:23-23
Wives, submit yourselves unto your own husbands, as unto the Lord.
23 For the husband is the head of the wife, even as Christ is the head
of the church: and he is the saviour of the body.

Ephesians 5:25
Husbands, love your wives, even as Christ also loved the church, and gave himself for it.

Ephesians 5:31-32
For this cause shall a man leave his father and mother, and shall be
joined unto his wife, and they two shall be one flesh.32 This is a great
mystery: but I speak concerning Christ and the church.

Ecclesiastes 9:9
Live joyfully with the wife whom thou lovest all the days of the life of thy vanity, which he hath given thee under the sun, all the days of thy vanity: for that is thy portion in this life, and in thy labour which thou takest under the sun.

Proverbs 5:15
Drink waters out of thine own cistern, and running waters out of thine own well.

Proverbs 5:18-20
Let thy fountain be blessed: and rejoice with the wife of thy youth.
19 Let her be as the loving hind and pleasant roe; let her breasts
satisfy thee at all times; and be thou ravished always with her love.20
And why wilt thou, my son, be ravished with a strange woman, and
embrace the bosom of a stranger?

1 Corinthians 7:3
Let the husband render unto the wife due benevolence: and likewise also the wife unto the husband.

Ephesians 5:26
So ought men to love their wives as their own bodies. He that loveth his wife loveth himself.

Ephesians 5:31
For this cause shall a man leave his father and mother, and shall be joined unto his wife, and they two shall be one flesh.

1Timothy 5:8
But if any provide not for his own, and specially for those of his own house, he hath denied the faith, and is worse than an infidel.

Colossians 3:18-19
Wives, submit yourselves unto your own husbands, as it is fit in the Lord. 19 Husbands, love your wives, and be not bitter against them.

1Peter 3:7
Likewise, ye husbands, dwell with them according to knowledge, giving honour unto the wife, as unto the weaker vessel, and as being heirs together of the grace of life; that your prayers be not hindered.

Titus 2:4-5
That they may teach the young women to be sober, to love their husbands, to love their children, 5 To be discreet, chaste, keepers at home, good, obedient to their own husbands, that the word of God be not blasphemed.

1Timothy 3:4 One that ruleth well his own house, having his children in subjection with all gravity.

Ephesians 6:4 And, ye fathers, provoke not your children to wrath: but bring them up in the nurture and admonition of the Lord.

1Peter 3:1-2
Likewise, ye wives, be in subjection to your own husbands; that, if any obey not the word, they also may without the word be won by the conversation of the wives; 2 While they behold your chaste conversation coupled with fear.

1Timothy 2:11-14
Let the woman learn in silence with all subjection.12 But I suffer not a woman to teach, nor to usurp authority over the man, but to be in silence. 13 For Adam was first formed, then Eve. 14 And Adam was not deceived, but the woman being deceived was in the transgression.

Proverbs 31:10-11; See also Proverbs 31:10-31 Who can find a virtuous woman? For her price is far above rubies. 11 The heart of her husband doth safely trust in her, so that he shall have no need of spoil.

Proverbs 31:30
Favour is deceitful, and beauty is vain: but a woman that feareth the LORD, she shall be praised.

1 Peter 3:3-4
Whose adorning let it not be that outward adorning of plaiting the hair, and of wearing of gold, or of putting on of apparel; 4 But let it be the hidden man of the heart, in that which is not corruptible, even the ornament of a meek and quiet spirit, which is in the sight of God of great price.

Galatians 5:15 But if ye bite and devour one another, take heed that ye be not consumed one of another.

Matthew 5:23-24
Therefore if thou bring thy gift to the altar, and there rememberest that thy brother hath ought against thee; 24 Leave there thy gift

before the altar, and go thy way; first be reconciled to thy brother, and then come and offer thy gift.

Romans 12:18 If it be possible, as much as lieth in you, live peaceably with all men.

Matthew 12:25
And Jesus knew their thoughts, and said unto them, Every kingdom divided against itself is brought to desolation; and every city or house divided against itself shall not stand.

2 Samuel 18:33
And the king was much moved, and went up to the chamber over the gate, and wept: and as he went, thus he said, O my son Absalom, my son, my son Absalom! Would God I had died for thee, O Absalom, my son, my son!

Husband/Wife
Marriage Relations

Sub subjects for better understanding

Marriage was instituted and designed by God.

Genesis 2:18-25

And the LORD God said, It is not good that the man should be
alone; I will make him an help meet for him. 19 And out of the
ground the LORD God formed every beast of the field, and every
fowl of the air; and brought them unto Adam to see what he would
call them: and whatsoever Adam called every living creature, that
was the name thereof. 20 And Adam gave names to all cattle, and
to the fowl of the air, and to every beast of the field; but for Adam
there was not found an help meet for him. 21 And the LORD God
caused a deep sleep to fall upon Adam, and he slept: and he took one
of his ribs, and closed up the flesh instead thereof; 22 And the rib,
which the LORD God had taken from man, made he a woman, and
brought her unto the man. 23 And Adam said, This is now bone of
my bones, and flesh of my flesh: she shall be called Woman, because
she was taken out of Man. 24 Therefore shall a man leave his father
and his mother, and shall cleave unto his wife: and they shall be one
flesh. 25 And they were both naked, the man and his wife, and were
not ashamed.

Both Husband and wife must promote companionship and intimacy, for it is the heart of marriage.

Genesis 2:18, 24

And the LORD God said, It is not good that the man should be alone; I will make him an help meet for him. "...Therefore shall a man leave his father and his mother, and shall cleave unto his wife: and they shall be one flesh."

The relationship between husband and wife is similar to that between Christ and the church.

Ephesians 5:23

For the husband is the head of the wife, even as Christ is the head of the church: and he is the saviour of the body.

Ephesians 5:31-32

For this cause shall a man leave his father and mother, and shall be joined unto his wife, and they two shall be one flesh. 32 This is a great mystery: but I speak concerning Christ and the church.

The husband is the head of the wife and the home.

Ephesians 5:23

For the husband is the head of the wife, even as Christ is the head of the church: and he is the saviour of the body.

Husbands must love their wives as Christ loved the church.

Ephesians 5:25-33

Husbands, love your wives, even as Christ also loved the church, and gave himself for it; 26 That he might sanctify and cleanse it with the washing of water by the word, 27 That he might present it to himself a glorious church, not having spot, or wrinkle, or any such thing; but that it should be holy and without blemish. 28 So ought men to love their wives as their own bodies. He that loveth his wife loveth himself. 29 For no man ever yet hated his own flesh; but nourisheth and cherisheth it, even as the Lord the church: 30 For we are members of his body, of his flesh, and of his bones. 31

For this cause shall a man leave his father and mother, and shall be joined unto his wife, and they two shall be one flesh.32 This is a great mystery: but I speak concerning Christ and the church. 33 Nevertheless let every one of you in particular so love his wife even as himself; and the wife see that she reverence her husband.

Husbands must exercise headship in love.
Colossians 3:19 Husbands, love your wives, and be not bitter against them.

Husbands must treat their wives with respect and as equal heirs of God's gift.
1Peter 3:7
Likewise, ye husbands, dwell with them according to knowledge, giving honour unto the wife, as unto the weaker vessel, and as being heirs together of the grace of life; that your prayers be not hindered.

The Husband must manage his own home well; he is the manager.
1Timothy 3:4 One that ruleth well his own house, having his children in subjection with all gravity.

The husband and father is primary responsible for training the children.
Ephesians 6:4
And, ye fathers, provoke not your children to wrath: but bring them up in the nurture and admonition of the Lord. [See also Child Training.]

God design for the wife is that of a helper suitable for man.
Genesis 2:18
And the LORD God said, It is not good that the man should be alone; I will make him an help meet for him.

Both husband and wife must seek to reflect the relationship between Christ and His church.
Ephesians 5:25, 32
"Husbands, love your wives, even as Christ also loved the church, and gave himself for it..." This is a great mystery: but I speak concerning Christ and the church.

A wife is to submit to her husband, as the church submits to Christ.
Ephesians 5:22-24 Wives, submit yourselves unto your own husbands, as unto the Lord. 23 For the husband is the head of the wife, even as Christ is the head of the church: and he is the saviour of the body. 24 Therefore as the church is subject unto Christ, so let the wives be to their own husbands in every thing.

Colossians 3:18 Wives, submit yourselves unto your own husbands, as it is fit in the Lord.

1Peter 3:1-2
Likewise, ye wives, be in subjection to your own husbands; that, if any obey not the word, they also may without the word be won by the conversation of the wives; 2 While they behold your chaste conversation coupled with fear.

A woman is not to exercise authority over a man.
1Timothy 2:11-14
Let the woman learn in silence with all subjection.12 But I suffer not a woman to teach, nor to usurp authority over the man, but to be in silence. 13 For Adam was first formed, then Eve. 14 And Adam was not deceived, but the woman being deceived was in the transgression.

The Bible gives a description of a wife of noble character, who uses her gifts faithfully.

Proverbs 31:10-11
Who can find a virtuous woman? For her price is far above rubies.
11 The heart of her husband doth safely trust in her, so that he shall
have no need of spoil.

The fear of the Lord is more important than physical beauty.

Proverbs 31:30
Favour is deceitful, and beauty is vain: but a woman that feareth the LORD, she shall be praised.

1 Peter 3:3-4
Whose adorning let it not be that outward adorning of plaiting the
hair, and of wearing of gold, or of putting on of apparel; 4 But let
it be the hidden man of the heart, in that which is not corruptible,
even the ornament of a meek and quiet spirit, which is in the sight
of God of great price.

Husband and wife must not fight and destroy each other.

Galatians 5:15 But if ye bite and devour one another, take heed that ye be not consumed one of another.

Both husband and wife must quickly pursue peace when trouble arises.

Matthew 5:23-24
Therefore if thou bring thy gift to the altar, and there remembers that
thy brother hath ought against thee; 24 Leave there thy gift before
the altar, and go thy way; first be reconciled to thy brother, and then
come and offer thy gift.

Romans 12:18 If it be possible, as much as lieth in you, live peaceably with all men.

A house divided against itself cannot stand.

Matthew 12:25

And Jesus knew their thoughts, and said unto them, every kingdom divided against itself is brought to desolation; and every city or house divided against itself shall not stand.

Keep loving those who are wayward.

2 Samuel 18:33

(David never lost his love for his son Absalom, who tried to kill him. When he learned of his death, he wept.) And the king was much moved, and went up to the chamber over the gate, and wept: and as he went, thus he said, O my son Absalom, my son, my son Absalom! Would God I had died for thee, O Absalom, my son, my son!

Parents Duties

Genesis 18:19
For I know him, that he will command his children and his household after him, and they shall keep the way of the LORD, to do justice and judgment; that the LORD may bring upon Abraham that which he hath spoken of him.

Psalms 78:4-7
We will not hide them from their children, showing to the generation
to come the praises of the LORD, and his strength, and his wonderful
works that he hath done. 5 For he established a testimony in Jacob,
and appointed a law in Israel, which he commanded our fathers,
that they should make them known to their children: 6 That the
generation to come might know them, even the children which
should be born; who should arise and declare them to their children:
7 That they might set their hope in God, and not forget the works
of God, but keep his commandments.

Deuteronomy 11:19
And ye shall teach them your children, speaking of them when thou sittest in thine house, and when thou walkest by the way, when thou liest down, and when thou risest up.

Exodus 13:8
And thou shalt show thy son in that day, saying, this is done because of that which the LORD did unto me when I came forth out of Egypt.

Proverbs 22:6 Train up a child in the way he should go: and when he is old, he will not depart from it.

Deuteronomy 4:9-10
Only take heed to thyself, and keep thy soul diligently, lest thou forget the things which thine eyes have seen, and lest they depart from thy heart all the days of thy life: but teach them thy sons, and thy sons' sons; 10 Specially the day that thou stoodest before the LORD thy God in Horeb, when the LORD said unto me, Gather me the people together, and I will make them hear my words, that they may learn to fear me all the days that they shall live upon the earth, and that they may teach their children.

Proverbs 29:17 Correct thy son, and he shall give thee rest; yea, he shall give delight unto thy soul.

Ephesians 6:4
And, ye fathers, provoke not your children to wrath: but bring them up in the nurture and admonition of the Lord.

Colossians 3:21 Fathers, provoke not your children to anger, lest they be discouraged.

Children

Acts 16:31 And they said, Believe on the Lord Jesus Christ, and thou shalt be saved, and thy house.

Acts 2:39 For the promise is unto you, and to your children, and to all that are afar off, *even* as many as the Lord our God shall call.

Isaiah 54:13 And all thy children *shall be* taught of the LORD; and great *shall be* the peace of thy children.

Isaiah 44:3
For I will pour water upon him that is thirsty, and floods upon the dry ground: I will pour my spirit upon thy seed, and my blessing upon thine offspring:

Mark 10:14-16
But when Jesus saw it, he was much displeased, and said unto them, suffer the little children to come unto me, and forbid them not: for of such is the kingdom of God. 15 Verily I say unto you, whosoever shall not receive the kingdom of God as a little child, he shall not enter therein. 16 And he took them up in his arms, put his hands upon them, and blessed them.

Psalms 127:3-5
Lo, children are an heritage of the LORD: and the fruit of the womb is his reward. 4 As arrows are in the hand of a mighty man; so are children of the youth. 5 Happy is the man that hath his quiver full

of them: they shall not be ashamed, but they shall speak with the enemies in the gate.

Psalms 128:3
Thy wife *shall be as a* fruitful vine by the sides of thine house: the children like olive plants round about thy table.

Psalms 107:41 Yet setteth he the poor on high from affliction, and maketh *him* families like a flock.

Job 21:11 They send forth their little ones like a flock, and their children dance.

Proverbs 17:6 Children's children *are* the crown of old men; and the glory of children *are* their fathers.

Child Training

Proverbs 3:11-12 "My son, despise not the chastening of the LORD; neither be weary of his correction: 12 For whom the LORD loveth he correcteth; even as a father the son in whom he delighteth."

Proverbs 13:24 "He that spareth his rod hateth his son: but he that loveth him chasteneth him betimes."

Proverbs 19:18 "Chasten thy son while there is hope, and let not thy soul spare for his crying."

Proverbs 22:6 "Train up a child in the way he should go: and when he is old, he will not depart from it."

Proverbs 22:15 "Foolishness is bound in the heart of a child; but the rod of correction shall drive it far from him."

Proverbs 23:13-14
"Withhold not correction from the child: for if thou beatest him with the rod, he shall not die. 14 Thou shalt beat him with the rod, and shalt deliver his soul from hell."

Proverbs 29:15 "The rod and reproof give wisdom: but a child left to himself bringeth his mother to shame."

Proverbs 29:17 "Correct thy son, and he shall give thee rest; yea, he shall give delight unto thy soul."

Jeremiah 2:30a "In vain have I smitten your children; they received no correction."

Proverbs 13:14 "The law of the wise is a fountain of life, to depart from the snares of death."

Colossians 3:21 "Fathers, provoke not your children to anger, lest they be discouraged."

Deuteronomy 6:7
"And thou shalt teach them diligently unto thy children, and shalt Talk of them when thou sittest in thine house, and when thou walkest by the way, and when thou liest down, and when thou risest up."

Isaiah 28:9-10 "Whom shall he teach knowledge? And whom shall he make to understand doctrine? Them that are weaned from the milk, and drawn from the breasts. 10 For precept must be upon precept, precept upon precept; line upon line, line upon line; here a little, and there a little."

Isaiah 54:13 "And all thy children shall be taught of the LORD; and great shall be the peace of thy children."

Children's Duties

Ephesians 6:1-3
Children, obey your parents in the Lord: for this is right. [2] Honor the father and mother; which is the first commandment with promise; that it may be well with thee, and thou mayest live long on the earth.

Colossians 3:20 Children, obey *your* parents in all things: for this is well pleasing unto the Lord.

Luke 18:20
Thou knowest the commandments, Do not commit adultery, Do no kill, Do not steal, Do not bear false witness, Honor thy father and thy mother.

Deuteronomy 27:16
Cursed *be* he that setteth light by his father or his mother. And all the people shall say, Amen.

Leviticus 19:3 Ye shall fear every man his mother, and his father, and keep my Sabbaths: *I am* the LORD your God.

Deuteronomy 5:16
Honour thy father and thy mother, as the LORD thy God Hath Commanded thee; that thy days may be prolonged, and that it may go well with thee, in the land which the LORD thy God giveth thee.

Proverbs 6:20 My son, keep thy father's commandment, and forsake not the law of thy mother.

Proverbs 13:1
A wise son *heareth* his father's instruction: but a scorner heareth no rebuke. A fool despiseth his father's instruction: but he that regardeth reproof is prudent.

Proverbs 20:11 Even a child is known by his doings, whether his work be pure, and whether it be right.

Proverbs 10:1 The proverbs of Solomon. A wise son maketh a glad father: but a foolish son is the heaviness of his mother.

Proverbs 1:10 My son, if sinners entice thee, consent thou not.

Proverbs 28:7 Whoso keepeth the law is a wise son: but he that is a companion of riotous men shameth his father.

Proverbs 8:32 Now therefore hearken unto me, 0 ye children: for blessed are they that keep my ways.

Proverbs 8:33 Hear instruction, and be wise, and refuse it not.

Proverbs 23:15 My son, if thine heart be wise, my heart shall rejoice, even mine.

Proverbs 23:16 Yea, my reins shall rejoice, when thy lips speak right things.

Proverbs 23:22 Hearken unto thy father that begat thee, and despise not thy mother when she is old.

Proverbs 23:24-26 The father of the righteous shall greatly rejoice: and he that begetteth a wise child shall have joy of him. 25 Thy father and thy mother shall be glad, and she that bare thee shall rejoice. 26 My son, give me thin heart, and let thine eyes observe my ways.

Youth

Ecclesiast 11:9-10
Rejoice, O young man, in thy youth; and let thy heart cheer thee in the days of thy youth, and walk in the ways of thine heart, and in the sight of thine eyes: but know thou that for all these things God will bring thee into judgment. 10 Therefore remove sorrow from thy heart, and put away evil from thy flesh: for childhood and youth are vanity.

Ecclesiast 12:1
Remember now thy Creator in the days of thy youth, while the evil days come not, nor the years draw nigh, when thou shalt say, I have no pleasure in them.

Proverbs 12:1
My son, forget not my law; but let thine heart keep my commandments: 2 For length of days, and long life, and peace, shall they add to thee. 3 Let not mercy and truth forsake thee: bind them about thy neck; write them upon the table of thine heart: 4 So shalt thou find favour and good understanding in the sight of God and man.

Proverbs 3:5-6
Trust in the LORD with all thine heart; and lean not unto thine own understanding. 6 In all thy ways acknowledge him, and he shall direct thy paths.

Proverbs 1:7 The fear of the LORD is the beginning of knowledge: but fools despise wisdom and instruction.

Proverbs 9:10-11
The fear of the LORD is the beginning of wisdom: and the knowledge of the holy is understanding. 11 For by me thy days shall be multiplied, and the years of thy life shall be increased.

Proverbs 15:33 The fear of the LORD is the instruction of wisdom; and before honour is humility.

Proverbs 1:7 The fear of the LORD is the beginning of knowledge: but fools despise wisdom and instruction.

Proverbs 13:13 Whoso despiseth the word shall be destroyed: but he that feareth the commandment shall be rewarded.

Proverbs 12:1 Whoso loveth instruction loveth knowledge: but he that hateth reproof is brutish.

Proverbs 13:18 Poverty and shame shall be to him that refuseth instruction: but he that regardeth reproof shall be honoured.

Proverbs 15:5 A fool despiseth his father's instruction: but he that regardeth reproof is prudent.

Proverbs 15:12 A scorner loveth not one that reproveth him: neither will he go unto the wise.

Proverbs 15:31-32
The ear that heareth the reproof of life abideth among the wise. 32 He that refuseth instruction despiseth his own soul: but he that heareth reproof getteth understanding.

Proverbs 13:24 He that spareth his rod hateth his son: but he that loveth him chasteneth him betimes.

Proverbs 1:10-19
My son, if sinners entice thee, consent thou not. 11 If they say, Come with us, let us lay wait for blood, let us lurk privily for the innocent without cause: 12 Let us swallow them up alive as the grave; and whole, as those that go down into the pit: 13 We shall find all precious substance, we shall fill our houses with spoil: 14 Cast in thy lot among us; let us all have one purse: 15 My son, walk not thou in the way with them; refrain thy foot from their path: 16 For their feet run to evil, and make haste to shed blood. 17 Surely in vain the net is spread in the sight of any bird. 18 And they lay wait for their own blood; they lurk privily for their own lives.19 So are the ways of every one that is greedy of gain; which taketh away the life of the owners thereof.

Proverbs 1:10 My son, if sinners entice thee, consent thou not.

Proverbs 1:15 My son, walk not thou in the way with them; refrain thy foot from their path:

Proverbs 4:14-15
Enter not into the path of the wicked, and go not in the way of evil men. 15 Avoid it, pass not by it, turn from it, and pass away

1 Corinthians 15:58 Therefore, my beloved brethren, be ye stedfast, unmoveable, always abounding in the work of the Lord, forasmuch as ye know that your labour is not in vain in the Lord.

Ephesians 6:10-18
Finally, my brethren, be strong in the Lord, and in the power of his might. 11 Put on the whole armour of God that ye may be able to stand against the wiles of the devil. 12 For we wrestle not against flesh and blood, but against principalities, against powers, against the rulers of the darkness of this world, against spiritual wickedness in high places. 13 Wherefore take unto you the whole armour of God, that ye may be able to withstand in the evil day, and having done all, to stand. 14 Stand therefore, having your loins girt about

with truth, and having on the breastplate of righteousness; 15 And your feet shod with the preparation of the gospel of peace; 16 Above all, taking the shield of faith, wherewith ye shall be able to quench all the fiery darts of the wicked. 17 And take the helmet of salvation, and the sword of the Spirit, which is the word of God: 18 Praying always with all prayer and supplication in the Spirit, and watching thereunto with all perseverance and supplication for all saints.

Ephesians 6:10-11
Finally, my brethren, be strong in the Lord, and in the power of his might. 11 Put on the whole armour of God, that ye may be able to stand against the wiles of the devil.

Genesis 39:9-10 There is none greater in this house than I; neither hath he kept back any thing from me but thee, because thou art his wife: how then can I do this great wickedness, and sin against God? 10 And it came to pass, as she spake to Joseph day by day, that he hearkened not unto her, to lie by her, or to be with her.

Daniel 1:8-9
But Daniel purposed in his heart that he would not defile himself with the portion of the king's meat, nor with the wine which he drank: therefore he requested of the prince of the eunuchs that he might not defile himself. 9 Now God had brought Daniel into favour and tender love with the prince of the eunuchs.

Daniel 6:10
Now when Daniel knew that the writing was signed, he went into his house; and his windows being open in his chamber toward Jerusalem, he kneeled upon his knees three times a day, and prayed, and gave thanks before his God, as he did aforetime.

Daniel 3:16-18
Shadrach, Meshach, and Abednego, answered and said to the king, O Nebuchadnezzar, we are not careful to answer thee in this matter. 17 If it be so, our God whom we serve is able to deliver us from the

burning fiery furnace, and he will deliver us out of thine hand, O king. 18 But if not, be it known unto thee, O king, that we will not serve thy gods, nor worship the golden image which thou hast set up.

Exodus 20:12
Honour thy father and thy mother: that thy days may be long upon the land which the LORD thy God giveth thee.

Ephesians 6:1-3
Children, obey your parents in the Lord: for this is right.2 Honour thy father and mother; which is the first commandment with promise; 3 That it may be well with thee, and thou mayest live long on the earth.

Colossians 3:20 Children, obey your parents in all things: for this is well pleasing unto the Lord.

2 Timothy 2:22 Flee also youthful lusts: but follow righteousness, faith, charity, peace, with them that call on the Lord out of a pure heart.

Divorce

Matthew 5:32
But I say unto you, that whosoever shall put away his wife, saving for the cause of fornication, causeth her to commit adultery: and whosoever shall marry her that is divorced committeth adultery.

Mark 10:11-12
And he saith unto them, whosoever shall put away his wife, and
marry another, committeth adultery against her. 12 And if a
woman shall put away her husband, and be married to another, she committeth adultery.

Romans 7:2-3
For the woman which hath an husband is bound by the law to her husband so long as he liveth; but if the husband be dead, she is loosed
from the law of her husband. 3 So then if, while her husband liveth,
she be married to another man, she shall be called an adulteress: but if her husband be dead, she is free from that law; so that she is no adulteress, though she be married to another man.

1Corinthians 7:11-39 But and if she depart, let her remain unmarried, or be reconciled to her husband: and let not the husband put away his wife…"

1Corinthians 7:15 But if the unbelieving depart, let him depart. A brother or a sister is not under bondage in such cases: but God hath called us to peace.

1Corinthians 7:27 Art thou bound unto a wife? Seek not to be loosed. Art thou loosed from a wife? Seek not a wife.

1Corinthians 7:28 But and if thou marry, thou hast not sinned; and if a virgin marry, she hath not sinned. Nevertheless such shall have trouble in the flesh: but I spare you.

1Corinthians 7:39 The wife is bound by the law as long as her husband liveth; but if her husband be dead, she is at liberty to be married to whom she will; only in the Lord.

[Do not hang on to your old life; if you were married and divorced before you were born again:]
2 Corinthians 5:17 Therefore if any man be in Christ, he is a new creature: old things are passed away; ***behold all things are become new.*** [Bold print my emphasis]

"Remember ye not the former things, neither consider the things of old. 19 Behold, I will do a new thing; now it shall spring forth; shall ye not know it? …" –Isaiah 43:18-19

Homosexual/Lesbian

Romans 1:24-27
Wherefore God also gave them up to uncleanness through the lusts of
their own hearts, to dishonour their own bodies between themselves:
25 Who changed the truth of God into a lie, and worshipped and
served the creature more than the Creator, who is blessed for ever.
Amen. 26 For this cause God gave them up unto vile affections:
for even their women did change the natural use into that which is
against nature. 27 And likewise also the men, leaving the natural use
of the woman, burned in their lust one toward another; men with
men working that which is unseemly, and receiving in themselves
that recompense of their error which was meet.

Jude 1:7
Even as Sodom and Gomorrha, and the cities about them in like manner, giving themselves over to fornication, and going after strange flesh, are set forth for an example, suffering the vengeance of eternal fire.

Leviticus 20:13 If a man also lie with mankind, as he lieth with a woman, both of them have committed an abomination: they shall surely be put to death; their blood shall be upon them.

Leviticus 18:22 Thou shalt not lie with mankind, as with womankind: it is abomination.

Romans 8:5-8
For they that are after the flesh do mind the things of the flesh; but they that are after the Spirit the things of the Spirit. 6 For to be carnally minded is death; but to be spiritually minded is life and peace. 7 Because the carnal mind is enmity against God: for it is not subject to the law of God, neither indeed can be. 8 So then they that are in the flesh cannot please God.

Galatia ns 5:19-21
Now the works of the flesh are manifest, which are these; Adultery, fornication, uncleanness, lasciviousness, 20 Idolatry, witchcraft, hatred, variance, emulations, wrath, strife, seditions, heresies, 21 Envyings, murders, drunkenness, revellings, and such like: of the which I tell you before, as I have also told you in time past, that they which do such things shall not inherit the kingdom of God.

1 Corinthians 6:9-11
Know ye not that the unrighteous shall not inherit the kingdom of God? Be not deceived: neither fornicators, nor idolaters, nor adulterers, nor effeminate **[ef-fem-i-nate- An offensive term used to describe a man whose behavior, appearance, or speech is considered to be similar to that traditionally associated with women or girls]. [Today they are referred to as Homosexual/Lesbian. See Romans 1:24-27, Jude 1:7, Leviticus 20:13, Leviticus 18:22, Romans 8:5-8, Galatians 5:19-21**] nor abusers of themselves with mankind, 10 Nor thieves, nor covetous, nor drunkards, nor revilers, nor extortioners, shall inherit the kingdom of God. 11 And such were some of you: but ye are washed, but ye are sanctified, but ye are justified in the name of the Lord Jesus, and by the Spirit of our God.

Romans 1:24-27
Wherefore God also gave them up to uncleanness through the lusts of their own hearts, to dishonour their own bodies between themselves: 25 Who changed the truth of God into a lie, and worshipped and served the creature more than the Creator, who is blessed for ever. Amen. 26 **For this cause God gave them up unto**

vile affections: for even their women did change the natural use into that which is against nature. 27 And likewise also the men, leaving the natural use of the woman, burned in their lust one toward another; men with men working that which is unseemly, and receiving in themselves that recompense of their error which was meet. [Bold print my emphasis]

Romans 7:23-25
But I see another law in my members, warring against the law of my mind, and bringing me into captivity to the law of sin which is in my members. 24 O wretched man that I am! Who shall deliver me from the body of this death? 25 I thank God through Jesus Christ our Lord. So then with the mind I myself serve the law of God; but with the flesh the law of sin.

Romans 6:19 Knowing that Christ being raised from the dead dieth no more; death hath no more dominion over him.

Galatians 5:16 This I say then, Walk in the Spirit, and ye shall not fulfil the lust of the flesh.

1Peter 4:1-3 Forasmuch then as Christ hath suffered for us in the flesh, arm yourselves likewise with the same mind: for he that hath suffered in the flesh hath ceased from sin; 2 That he no longer should live the rest of his time in the flesh to the lusts of men, but to the will of God. 3 For the time past of our life may suffice us to have wrought the will of the Gentiles, when we walked in lasciviousness, lusts, excess of wine, revellings, banquetings, and abominable idolatries:

James 4:17 Therefore to him that knoweth to do good, and doeth it not, to him it is sin.

Psalms 141:4 Incline not my heart to any evil thing, to practice wicked works with men that work iniquity: and let me not eat of their dainties.

Romans 12:1-2
Beseech you therefore, brethren, by the mercies of God, that ye present your bodies a living sacrifice, holy, acceptable unto God, which is your reasonable service. 2 And be not conformed to this world: but be ye transformed by the renewing of your mind, that ye may prove what is that good, and acceptable, and perfect, will of God.

1 Thessalonians 4:1-8
Furthermore then we beseech you, brethren, and exhort you by the Lord Jesus, that as ye have received of us how ye ought to walk and to please God, so ye would abound more and more. 2 For ye know what commandments we gave you by the Lord Jesus. 3 For this is the will of God, even your sanctification, that ye should abstain from fornication: 4 That every one of you should know how to possess his vessel in sanctification and honour; 5 Not in the lust of concupiscence, even as the Gentiles which know not God: 6 That no man go beyond and defraud his brother in any matter: because that the Lord is the avenger of all such, as we also have forewarned you and testified. 7 For God hath not called us unto uncleanness, but unto holiness. 8 He therefore that despiseth, despiseth not man, but God, who hath also given unto us his Holy Spirit.

Quick Reference
A-W

Counseling with God's Word

Adultery

1 Corinthians 6:9-10
Know ye not that the unrighteous shall not inherit the kingdom of God? Be not deceived: neither fornicators, nor idolaters, nor adulterers, nor effeminate, nor abusers of themselves with mankind,
10 Nor thieves, nor covetous, nor drunkards, nor revilers, nor extortioners, shall inherit the kingdom of God.

Exodus 20:14 You shall not commit adultery.

Matthew 5:28 But I say unto you, that whosoever looketh on a woman to lust after her hath committed adultery with her already in his heart.

Matthew 15:19 For out of the heart proceed evil thoughts, murders, adulteries, fornications, thefts, false witness, blasphemies.

Proverbs 5:20 And why wilt thou, my son, be ravished with a strange woman, and embrace the bosom of a stranger?

Hebrews 13:4 Marriage is honourable in all, and the bed undefiled: but whoremongers and adulterers God will judge.

Proverbs 4:23 Keep thy heart with all diligence; for out of it are the issues of life.

Proverbs 4:13 Take fast hold of instruction; let her not go: keep her; for she is thy life…"

Proverbs 6:27-28 Can a man take fire in his bosom, and his clothes not be burned? 28 Can one go upon hot coals, and his feet not be burned?

Proverbs 6:20-35
My son, keep thy father's commandment, and forsake not the law of thy mother: 21 Bind them continually upon thine heart, and tie them about thy neck. 22 When thou goest, it shall lead thee; when thou sleepest, it shall keep thee; and when thou awakest, it shall talk with thee. 23 For the commandment is a lamp; and the law is light; and reproofs of instruction are the way of life: 24 To keep thee from the evil woman, from the flattery of the tongue of a strange woman. 25 Lust not after her beauty in thine heart; neither let her take thee with her eyelids. 26 For by means of a whorish woman a man is brought to a piece of bread: and the adulteress will hunt for the precious life. 27 Can a man take fire in his bosom, and his clothes not be burned? 28 Can one go upon hot coals, and his feet not be burned? 29 So he that goeth in to his neighbour's wife; whosoever toucheth her shall not be innocent. 30 Men do not despise a thief, if he steal to satisfy his soul when he is hungry; 31 But if he be found, he shall restore sevenfold; he shall give all the substance of his house. 32 But whoso committeth adultery with a woman lacketh understanding: he that doeth it destroyeth his own soul. 33 A wound and dishonour shall he get; and his reproach shall not be wiped away. 34 For jealousy is the rage of a man: therefore he will not spare in the day of vengeance. 35 He will not regard any ransom; neither will he rest content, though thou givest many gifts.

Proverbs 7:1-27
My son, keep my words, and lay up my commandments with thee. 2 Keep my commandments, and live; and my law as the apple of thine eye. 3 Bind them upon thy fingers, write them upon the table of thine heart. 4 Say unto wisdom, Thou art my sister; and call

understanding thy kinswoman: 5 That they may keep thee from the strange woman, from the stranger which flattereth with her words... "

Proverbs 22:14 The mouth of strange women is a deep pit: he that is abhorred of the LORD shall fall therein.

Proverbs 23:26-28 My son, give me thine heart, and let thine eyes observe my ways. 27 For a whore is a deep ditch; and a strange woman is a narrow pit. 28 She also lieth in wait as for a prey, and increaseth the transgressors among men.

1Corinthian 6:11
And such were some of you: but ye are washed, but ye are sanctified, but ye are justified in the name of the Lord Jesus, and by the Spirit of our God.

Matthew 5:27-30
Ye have heard that it was said by them of old time, Thou shalt not commit adultery: 28 But I say unto you, That whosoever looketh on a woman to lust after her hath committed adultery with her already in his heart. 29 And if thy right eye offend thee, pluck it out, and cast it from thee: for it is profitable for thee that one of thy members should perish, and not that thy whole body should be cast into hell. 30 And if thy right hand offend thee, cut it off, and cast it from thee: for it is profitable for thee that one of thy members should perish, and not that thy whole body should be cast into hell.

Matthew 5:31-32 "... Whosoever shall put away his wife, let him give her a writing of divorcement: 32 But I say unto you, That whosoever shall put away his wife, saving for the cause of fornication, causeth her to commit adultery: and whosoever shall marry her that is divorced committeth adultery."

Matthew 19:9 And I say unto you, Whosoever shall put away his wife, except it be for fornication, and shall marry another, committeth adultery: and whoso marrieth her which is put away doth commit adultery.

Romans 8:5-6 For they that are after the flesh do mind the things of the flesh; but they that are after the Spirit the things of the Spirit. 6 For to be carnally minded is death; but to be spiritually minded is life and peace.

Romans 12:1-2
I beseech you therefore, brethren, by the mercies of God, that ye present your bodies a living sacrifice, holy, acceptable unto God, which is your reasonable service. 2 And be not conformed to this world: but be ye transformed by the renewing of your mind, that ye may prove what is that good, and acceptable, and perfect, will of God.

Proverbs 2:16-18
To deliver thee from the strange woman, even from the stranger which flattereth with her words; 17 Which forsaketh the guide of her youth, and forgetteth the covenant of her God. 18 For her house inclineth unto death, and her paths unto the dead.

Alcohol/Drug Abuse

1Corinthians 6:15
Know ye not that your bodies are the members of Christ? Shall I then take the members of Christ, and make them the members of an harlot? God forbid.

1 Corinthians 6:19-20
What? Know ye not that your body is the temple of the Holy Ghost which is in you, which ye have of God, and ye are not your own? 20 For ye are bought with a price: therefore glorify God in your body, and in your spirit, which are God's.

Luke 21:34 And take heed to yourselves, lest at any time your hearts be overcharged with surfeiting, and drunkenness, and cares of this life, and so that day come upon you unawares.

Proverbs 20:1 Wine is a mocker, strong drink is raging: and whosoever is deceived thereby is not wise

Proverbs 21:17 He that loveth pleasure shall be a poor man: he that loveth wine and oil shall not be rich.

Proverbs 23:29-35
Who hath woe? Who hath sorrow? Who hath contentions? Who hath babbling? Who hath wounds without cause? Who hath redness of eyes? 30 They that tarry long at the wine; they that go to seek mixed wine. 31 Look not thou upon the wine when it is red, when

it giveth his colour in the cup, when it moveth itself aright. 32 At the last it biteth like a serpent, and stingeth like an adder. 33 Thine eyes shall behold strange women, and thine heart shall utter perverse things. 34 Yea, thou shalt be as he that lieth down in the midst of the sea, or as he that lieth upon the top of a mast. 35 They have stricken me, shalt thou say, and I was not sick; they have beaten me, and I felt it not: when shall I awake? I will seek it yet again.

Proverbs 23:32-35 At the last it biteth like a serpent, and stingeth like an adder. 33 Thine eyes shall behold strange women, and thine heart shall utter perverse things. 34 Yea, thou shalt be as he that lieth down in the midst of the sea, or as he that lieth upon the top of a mast. 35 They have stricken me, shalt thou say, and I was not sick; they have beaten me, and I felt it not: when shall I awake? I will seek it yet again.

Isaiah 28:1-4
Woe to the crown of pride, to the drunkards of Ephraim, whose glorious beauty is a fading flower, which are on the head of the fat valleys of them that are overcome with wine! :2 Behold, the Lord hath a mighty and strong one, which as a tempest of hail and a destroying storm, as a flood of mighty waters overflowing, shall cast down to the earth with the hand. 3 The crown of pride, the drunkards of Ephraim, shall be trodden under feet: 4 And the glorious beauty, which is on the head of the fat valley, shall be a fading flower, and as the hasty fruit before the summer; which when he that looketh upon it seeth, while it is yet in his hand he eateth it up.

Ephesians 5:15-18
See then that ye walk circumspectly, not as fools, but as wise, 16 Redeeming the time, because the days are evil. 17 Wherefore be ye not unwise, but understanding what the will of the Lord is.18 And be not drunk with wine, wherein is excess; but be filled with the Spirit;

1Corinthians 6:9-10 Know ye not that the unrighteous shall not inherit the kingdom of God? Be not deceived: neither fornicators, nor idolaters, nor adulterers, nor effeminate, nor abusers of themselves with mankind, 10 Nor thieves, nor covetous, nor drunkards, nor revilers, nor extortioners, shall inherit the kingdom of God.

1Corinthians 6:11 And such were some of you: but ye are washed, but ye are sanctified, but ye are justified in the name of the Lord Jesus, and by the Spirit of our God.

1 Corinthians 5:11 But now I have written unto you not to keep company, if any man that is called a brother be a fornicator, or covetous, or an idolater, or a railer, or a drunkard, or an extortioner; with such an one no not to eat.

Proverbs 23:19-20 Hear thou, my son, and be wise, and guide thine heart in the way. 20 Be not among winebibbers; among riotous eaters of flesh:

Anger

Psalm 7:11 God judgeth the righteous, and God is angry with the wicked every day. [God was angry with the wicked.]

1 Kings 11:9 And the LORD was angry with Solomon, because his heart was turned from the LORD God of Israel, which had appeared unto him twice. [God was angry with Solomon.]

2 Kings 17:18 Therefore the LORD was very angry with Israel, and removed them out of his sight: there was none left but the tribe of Judah only. [God was angry with Israel.]

Mark 3:5
And when he had looked round about on them with anger, being grieved for the hardness of their hearts, he saith unto the man, Stretch forth thine hand. And he stretched it out: and his hand was restored whole as the other. [Jesus was angry with the Pharisees]

Job 5:2 For wrath killeth the foolish man, and envy slayeth the silly one.

Psalm 18:48 He delivereth me from mine enemies: yea, thou liftest me up above those that rise up against me: thou hast delivered me from the violent man.

Psalm 68:6 God setteth the solitary in families: he bringeth out those which are bound with chains: but the rebellious dwell in a dry land.

Proverbs 10:12 Hatred stirreth up strifes: but love covereth all sins.

Proverbs 12:16 A fool's wrath is presently known: but a prudent man covereth shame.

Colossians 3:8 But now ye also put off all these; anger, wrath, malice, blasphemy, filthy communication out of your mouth.

Ephesians 4:31-32 Let all bitterness, and wrath, and anger, and clamour, and evil speaking, be put away from you, with all malice:
32 And be ye kind one to another, tenderhearted, forgiving one another, even as God for Christ's sake hath forgiven you.

Proverbs 29:11 A fool uttereth all his mind: but a wise man keepeth it in till afterwards.

Jonah 4:4, 9 Then said the LORD, Doest thou well to be angry? "... And God said to Jonah," "Doest thou well to be angry for the gourd?" And he said, "I do well" to be angry, "even unto death."

Proverbs 14:17 He that is soon angry dealeth foolishly: and a man of wicked devices is hated.

Proverbs 20:3 It is an honour for a man to cease from strife: but every fool will be meddling.

Proverbs 15:1 A soft answer turneth away wrath: but grievous words stir up anger.

Proverbs 15:18 A wrathful man stirreth up strife: but he that is slow to anger appeaseth strife.

Proverbs 16:32 He that is slow to anger is better than the mighty; and he that ruleth his spirit than he that taketh a city.

Proverbs 17:9 He that covereth a transgression seeketh love; but he that repeateth a matter separateth very friends.

Proverbs 19:11 The discretion of a man deferreth his anger; and it is his glory to pass over a transgression.

Proverbs 21:19 It is better to dwell in the wilderness, than with a contentious and an angry woman.

Proverbs 25:28 He that hath no rule over his own spirit is like a city that is broken down, and without walls.

Proverbs 29:22 An angry man stirreth up strife, and a furious man aboundeth in transgression.

Proverbs 29:23 A man's pride shall bring him low: but honour shall uphold the humble in spirit.

Proverbs 30:33 Surely the churning of milk bringeth forth butter, and the wringing of the nose bringeth forth blood: so the forcing of wrath bringeth forth strife.

Ecclesiastes 7:9 Better is the end of a thing than the beginning thereof: and the patient in spirit is better than the proud in spirit.

Ephesians 4:26 Be ye angry, and sin not: let not the sun go down upon your wrath:

Proverbs 4:27 Neither give place to the devil.

Ephesians 4:31 Let all bitterness, and wrath, and anger, and clamour, and evil speaking, be put away from you, with all malice:

Ephesians 4:32 Be ye kind one to another, tenderhearted, forgiving one another, even as God for Christ's sake hath forgiven you.

James 1:19 Wherefore, my beloved brethren, let every man be swift to hear, slow to speak, slow to wrath:

James 1:20 For the wrath of man worketh not the righteousness of God.

Galatians 5:19-21
Now the works of the flesh are manifest, which are these; Adultery, fornication, uncleanness, lasciviousness, 20 Idolatry, witchcraft, hatred, variance, emulations, wrath, strife, seditions, heresies, 21 Envyings, murders, drunkenness, revellings, and such like: of the which I tell you before, as I have also told you in time past, that they which do such things shall not inherit the kingdom of God.

Galatians 5:22-25
But the fruit of the Spirit is love, joy, peace, longsuffering, gentleness, goodness, faith, 23 Meekness, temperance: against such there is no law. 24 And they that are Christ's have crucified the flesh with the affections and lusts. 25 If we live in the Spirit, let us also walk in the Spirit.

Matthew 5:21-22
Ye have heard that it was said by them of old time, Thou shalt not kill; and whosoever shall kill shall be in danger of the judgment: 22 But I say unto you, That whosoever is angry with his brother without a cause shall be in danger of the judgment: and whosoever shall say to his brother, Raca, shall be in danger of the council: but whosoever shall say, Thou fool, shall be in danger of hell fire.

Anxiety/Worry

Proverbs 12:25 Heaviness in the heart of man maketh it stoop: but a good word maketh it glad.

Psalms 107:9 For he satisfieth the longing soul, and filleth the hungry soul with goodness.

Matthew 6:34 Take therefore no thought for the morrow: for the morrow shall take thought for the things of itself. Sufficient unto the day is the evil thereof.

Matthew 28:20 "…, I am with you alway, even unto the end of the world. Amen.

Luke 12:31 But rather seek ye the kingdom of God; and all these things shall be added unto you.

Philippians 4:6-7
Be careful for nothing; but in every thing by prayer and supplication with thanksgiving let your requests be made known unto God. 7 And the peace of God, which passeth all understanding, shall keep your hearts and minds through Christ Jesus.

Ephesians 3:11-12 According to the eternal purpose which he purposed in Christ Jesus our Lord: 12 In whom we have boldness and access with confidence by the faith of him.

1Peter 5:7 Casting all your care upon him; for he careth for you.

Isaiah 41:10, 13
Fear thou not; for I am with thee: be not dismayed; for I am thy God: I will strengthen thee; yea, I will help thee; yea, I will uphold thee with the right hand of my righteousness. "…For I the LORD thy God will hold thy right hand, saying unto thee, Fear not; I will help thee."

Philippians 4:8
Finally, brethren, whatsoever things are true, whatsoever things are honest, whatsoever things are just, whatsoever things are pure, whatsoever things are lovely, whatsoever things are of good report; if there be any virtue, and if there be any praise, think on these things.

2 Corinthians 12:9-10
And he said unto me, my grace is sufficient for thee: for my strength is made perfect in weakness. Most gladly therefore will I rather glory in my infirmities, that the power of Christ may rest upon me. 10 Therefore I take pleasure in infirmities, in reproaches, in necessities, in persecutions, in distresses for Christ's sake: for when I am weak, then am I strong.

Psalms 139:16 Thine eyes did see my substance, yet being unperfect; and in thy book all my members were written, which in continuance were fashioned, when as yet there was none of them.

Isaiah 44:6 Thus saith the LORD the King of Israel, and his redeemer the LORD of hosts; I am the first, and I am the last; and beside me there is no God.

Isaiah 45:5-7
Am the LORD, and there is none else, there is no God beside me: I girded thee, though thou hast not known me: 6 That they may know from the rising of the sun, and from the west, that there is

none beside me. I am the LORD, and there is none else. 7 I form the light, and create darkness: I make peace, and create evil: I the LORD do all these things.

Romans 8:28 And we know that all things work together for good to them that love God, to them who are the called according to his purpose.

John 14:1-3
Let not your heart be troubled: ye believe in God, believe also in me. 2 In my Father's house are many mansions: if it were not so, I would have told you. I go to prepare a place for you. 3 And if I go and prepare a place for you, I will come again, and receive you unto myself; that where I am, there ye may be also.

Isaiah 26:3-4 Thou wilt keep him in perfect peace, whose mind is stayed on thee: because he trusteth in thee. 4 Trust ye in the LORD for ever: for in the LORD JEHOVAH is everlasting strength:

Philippians 4:8 But seek ye first the kingdom of God, and his righteousness; and all these there be any praise, think on these things.

2 Corinthians 12:9-10
And he said unto me, my grace is sufficient for thee: for my strength is made perfect in weakness. Most gladly therefore will I rather glory in my infirmities, that the power of Christ may rest upon me. 10 Therefore I take pleasure in infirmities, in reproaches, in necessities, in persecutions, in distresses for Christ's sake: for when I am weak, then am I strong.

Psalms 139:16 Thine eyes did see my substance, yet being unperfect; and in thy book all my members were written, which in continuance were fashioned, when as yet there was none of them.

Isaiah 44:6 Thus saith the LORD the King of Israel, and his redeemer the LORD of hosts; I am the first, and I am the last; and beside me there is no God.

Isaiah 45:5-7
Am the LORD, and there is none else, there is no God beside me: I girded thee, though thou hast not known me: 6 That they may know from the rising of the sun, and from the west, that there is none beside me. I am the LORD, and there is none else. 7 I form the light, and create darkness: I make peace, and create evil: I the LORD do all these things.

Romans 8:28 And we know that all things work together for good to them that love God, to them who are the called according to his purpose.

John 14:1-3
Let not your heart be troubled: ye believe in God, believe also in me. 2 In my Father's house are many mansions: if it were not so, I would have told you. I go to prepare a place for you. 3 And if I go and prepare a place for you, I will come again, and receive you unto myself; that where I am, there ye may be also.

Isaiah 26:3-4 Thou wilt keep him in perfect peace, whose mind is stayed on thee: because he trusteth in thee. 4 Trust ye in the LORD for ever: for in the LORD JEHOVAH is everlasting strength:

Matthew 6:33-34
But seek ye first the kingdom of God, and his righteousness; and all these things shall be added unto you. 34 Take therefore no thought for the morrow: for the morrow shall take thought for the things of itself. Sufficient unto the day is the evil thereof.

Belief

John 3:16 For God so loved the world, that he gave his only begotten Son, that whosoever believeth in him should not perish, but have everlasting life.

Acts 10:43 "… All the prophets' witness, that through his name whosoever believeth in him shall receive remission of sins.

Romans 9:33 As it is written, Behold, I lay in Sion a stumblingstone and rock of offence: and whosoever believeth on him shall not be ashamed.

Romans 10:9 That if thou shalt confess with thy mouth the Lord Jesus, and shalt believe in thine heart that God hath raised him from the dead, thou shalt be saved.

John 1:12 But as many as received him, to them gave he power to become the sons of God, even to them that believe on his name:

John 3:18 He that believeth on him is not condemned: but he that believeth not is condemned already, because he hath not believed in the name of the only begotten Son of God.

John 3:36 He that believeth on the Son hath everlasting life: and he that believeth not the Son shall not see life; but the wrath of God abideth on him.

1 Peter 2:6 Wherefore also it is contained in the scripture, Behold, I lay in Sion a chief corner stone, elect, precious: and he that believeth on him shall not be confounded.

Acts 16:31 And they said, Believe on the Lord Jesus Christ, and thou shalt be saved, and thy house.

John 12:46 I am come a light into the world, that whosoever believeth on me should not abide in darkness.

John 6:35 And Jesus said unto them, I am the bread of life: he that cometh to me shall never hunger; and he that believeth on me shall never thirst.

Mark 9:23 Jesus said unto him, If thou canst believe, all things are possible to him that believeth.

John 20:29 Jesus saith unto him, Thomas, because thou hast seen me, thou hast believed: blessed are they that have not seen, and yet have believed.

John 6:47 Verily, verily, I say unto you, He that believeth on me hath everlasting life.

Mark 1:15 And saying, the time is fulfilled, and the kingdom of God is at hand: repent ye, and believe the gospel.

Acts 18:8 And Crispus, the chief ruler of the synagogue, believed on the Lord with all his house; and many of the Corinthians hearing believed, and were baptized.

John 2:11 This beginning of miracles did Jesus in Cana of Galilee, and manifested forth his glory; and his disciples believed on him.

John 4:39 And many of the Samaritans of that city believed on him for the saying of the woman, which testified, He told me all that ever I did.

John 7:31 And many of the people believed on him, and said, When Christ cometh, will he do more miracles than these which this man hath done?
John 7:48 Have any of the rulers or of the Pharisees believed on him?

John 8:30 As he spake these words, many believed on him.

John 6:35 And Jesus said unto them, I am the bread of life: he that cometh to me shall never hunger; and he that believeth on me shall never thirst.

Mark 9:23 Jesus said unto him, If thou canst believe, all things are possible to him that believeth.

John 20:29 Jesus saith unto him, Thomas, because thou hast seen me, thou hast believed: blessed are they that have not seen, and yet have believed.

John 6:47 Verily, verily, I say unto you, He that believeth on me hath everlasting life.

Mark 1:15 And saying, the time is fulfilled, and the kingdom of God is at hand: repent ye, and believe the gospel.

Acts 18:8 And Crispus, the chief ruler of the synagogue, believed on the Lord with all his house; and many of the Corinthians hearing believed, and were baptized.

John 2:11 This beginning of miracles did Jesus in Cana of Galilee, and manifested forth his glory; and his disciples believed on him.

John 4:39 And many of the Samaritans of that city believed on him for the saying of the woman, which testified, He told me all that ever I did.

John 7:31 And many of the people believed on him, and said, When Christ cometh, will he do more miracles than these which this man hath done?

John 7:48 Have any of the rulers or of the Pharisees believed on him?

John 8:30 As he spake these words, many believed on him.

Charity

Psalms 41:1-2
"...Blessed is he that considereth the poor: the LORD will deliver him in time of trouble. 2 The LORD will preserve him, and keep him alive; and he shall be blessed upon the earth: and thou wilt not deliver him unto the will of his enemies."

Proverbs 19:17 He that hath pity upon the poor lendeth unto the LORD; and that which he hath given will he pay him again.

Luke 14:13-14 But when thou makest a feast, call the poor, the maimed, the lame, the blind: 14 And thou shalt be blessed; for they cannot recompense thee: for thou shalt be recompensed at the resurrection of the just.

Luke 12:33 Sell that ye have, and give alms; provide yourselves bags which wax not old, a treasure in the heavens that faileth not, where no thief approacheth, neither moth corrupteth.

Proverbs 14:21 He that despiseth his neighbour sinneth: but he that hath mercy on the poor, happy is he.

Ecclesiastes 11:1 Cast thy bread upon the waters: for thou shalt find it after many days.

Psalms 112:9 He hath dispersed, he hath given to the poor; his righteousness endureth for ever; his horn shall be exalted with honour.

Proverbs 22:9 He that hath a bountiful eye shall be blessed; for he giveth of his bread to the poor.

Luke 6:38
Give, and it shall be given unto you; good measure, pressed down, and shaken together, and running over, shall men give into your bosom. For with the same measure that ye mete withal it shall be measured to you again.

Proverbs 28:27 He that giveth unto the poor shall not lack: but he that hideth his eyes shall have many a curse.

2 Corinthians 9:7 Every man according as he purposeth in his heart, so let him give; not grudgingly, or of necessity: for God loveth a cheerful giver.

Proverbs 11:24-25
There is that scattereth, and yet increaseth; and there is that withholdeth more than is meet, but it trended to poverty. 25 The liberal soul shall be made fat: and he that watereth shall be watered also himself.

Psalms 37:25-26 Have been young, and now am old; yet have I not seen the righteous forsaken, nor his seed begging bread. 26 He is ever merciful, and lendeth; and his seed is blessed.

Isaiah 58:10 And if thou draw out thy soul to the hungry, and satisfy the afflicted soul; then shall thy light rise in obscurity, and thy darkness be as the noon day.

1Timothy 6:17-18
Charge them that are rich in this world, that they be not highminded, nor trust in uncertain riches, but in the living God, who giveth us richly all things to enjoy; 18 That they do good, that they be rich in good works, ready to distribute, willing to communicate.

Isaiah 58:7-8 Is it not to deal thy bread to the hungry, and that thou bring the poor that are cast out to thy house? When thou seest the naked, that thou cover him; and that thou hide not thyself from thine own flesh? Then shall thy light break forth as the morning, and thine health shall spring forth speedily: and thy righteousness shall go before thee; the glory of the LORD shall be thy reward.

Deuteronomy 14:29
And the Levite, (because he hath no part nor inheritance with thee,) and the stranger, and the fatherless, and the widow, which are within thy gates, shall come, and shall eat and be satisfied; that The LORD thy God may bless thee in all the work of thine hand which thou doest.

Mark 10:21
Then Jesus beholding him loved him, and said unto him, one thing thou lackest: go thy way, sell whatsoever thou hast, and give to the poor, and thou shalt have treasure in heaven: and come, take up the cross, and follow me.

Matthew 6:1-4
Take heed that ye do not your alms before men, to be seen of them: otherwise ye have no reward of your Father which is in heaven. Therefore when thou doest thine alms, do not sound a trumpet before thee, as the hypocrites do in the synagogues and in the streets, that they may have glory of men. Verily I say unto you, They have their reward. 3 But when thou doest alms, let not thy left hand know what thy right hand doeth: 4 That thine alms may be in secret: and thy Father which seeth in secret himself shall reward thee openly.

Matthew 25:34-40
Then shall the King say unto them on his right hand, Come, ye blessed of my Father, inherit the kingdom prepared for you from the foundation of the world: 35 For I was an hungered, and ye gave me meat: I was thirsty, and ye gave me drink: I was a stranger, and ye took me in: 36 Naked, and ye clothed me: I was sick, and ye

visited me: I was in prison, and ye came unto me. Then shall the
righteous answer him, saying, Lord, when saw we thee an hungered,
and fed thee? Or thirsty, and gave thee drink? 38 When saw we thee
a stranger, and took thee in? or naked, and clothed thee? Or when
saw we thee sick, or in prison, and came unto thee? And the King
shall answer and say unto them, Verily I say unto you, Inasmuch as
ye have done it unto one of the least of these my brethren, ye have
done it unto me.

Church

Matthew 16:18 And I say also unto thee, that thou art Peter, and upon this rock I will build my church; and the gates of hell shall not prevail against it.

Colossians 1:18 And he is the head of the body, the church: who is the beginning, the, firstborn from the dead; that in all *things* he might have the preeminence.

Ephesians 1:22 And hath put all *things* under his feet, and gave him *to be* the head over all *things* to the church.

Ephesians 3:10 To the intent that now unto the principalities and powers in heavenly; *places* might be known by the church the manifold wisdom of God.

Acts 2:47 Praising God, and having favour with all the people. And the Lord added to the church daily such as should be saved.

Ephesians 3:21 Unto him *be* glory in the church by Christ Jesus throughout all ages world without end. Amen.

Ephesians 5:23 For the husband is the head of the wife, even as Christ is the head of the church: and he is the saviour of the body.

Ephesians 5:24 Therefore as the church is subject unto Christ, so *let* the wives *be* to, their own husbands in every thing.

Ephesians 5:25 Husbands, love your wives, even as Christ also loved the church, and gave himself for it.

Ephesians 5:27 That he might present it to himself a glorious church, not having spot, or wrinkle, or any such thing; but that it should be holy and without blemish.

Ephesians 5:29 For no man ever yet hated his own flesh; but nourisheth and cherisheth it, even as the Lord the church.

Timothy 3:5 (For if a man know not how to rule his own house, how shall he take care of the church of God?)

Acts 13:1
Now there were in the church that was at Antioch certain prophets and teachers; as Barnabas, and Simeon that was called Niger, and Lucius of Cyrene, and Manaen, which had been brought up with Herod the tetrarch, and Saul.

Acts 11:26
And when he had found him, he brought him unto Antioch. And it came to pass, that a whole year they assembled themselves with the church, and taught much people. And the disciples were called Christians first in Antioch.

Ephesians 4:11 And he gave some, apostles; and some, prophets; and some, evangelists; and some, pastors and teachers.

Ephesians 4:12 For the perfecting of the saints, for the work of the ministry, for the edifying of the body of Christ.

Ephesians 4:13 Till we all come in the unity of the faith, and of the knowledge of the Son of God, unto a perfect man, unto the measure of the stature of the fullness of Christ:

Ephesians 4:15 But speaking the truth in love, may grow up into him in all things which is the head, *even* Christ.

Hebrews 12:23 To the general assembly and church of the firstborn, which are written in heaven, and to God the Judge of all, and to the spirits of just men made perfect.

James 5:14 Is any sick among you? let him call for the elders of the church; and let them pray over him, anointing him with oil in the name of the Lord.

1Corinthians 12:28 And God hath set some in the church, first apostles, secondarily prophets, thirdly teachers, after that miracles, then gifts of healings helps, governments, diversities of tongues.

Revelation 2:1 Unto the angel of the church of Ephesus write; these things saith he that holdeth the seven stars in his right hand, who walketh in the midst of the seven golden candlesticks.

Revelation 2:8 And unto the angel of the church in Smyrna write; these things saith the first and the last, which was dead, and is alive.

Revelation 2:12 And to the angel of the church in Pergamos write; these things saith he which hath the sharp sword with two edges.

Revelation 2:18 And unto the angel of the church in Thyatira write; These things saith the Son of God, who hath his eyes like unto a flame of fire, and his fee *are* like fine brass.

Revelation 3:1 And unto the angel of the church in Sardis write; These things saith h that hath the seven Spirits of God, and the seven stars; I know the works, that thou hast a name that thou livest, and art dead.

Revelation 3:7 And to the angel of the church in Philadelphia write; These things saith he that is holy, he that is true, he that hath the key of David, he the openeth, and no man shutteth; and shutteth, and no man openeth.

Revelation 3:14 And unto the angel of the church of the Laodiceans write; these thing saith the Amen, the faithful and true witness, the beginning of the creation of God.

What to Do after You Are Saved

1. Join a Bible teaching church.
2. Attend worship regularly.
3. Give yourself wholly unto the Lord.
4. Be sure to maintain fellowship with God and the Saints.
5. Trust God and His (Have faith in His) Word.
6. Give the Lord praise and thanksgiving for all things.
7. Live Holy unto the Lord.
8. Give your Tithes and Offerings unto the Lord for the work of the Ministry.
9. Continue in God's Word.

Comfort

Psalms 46:1-3
To the chief Musician for the sons of Korah, A Song upon Alamoth.
God is our refuge and strength, a very present help in trouble. 2
Therefore will not we fear, though the earth be removed, and though
the mountains be carried into the midst of the sea; 3 Though the
waters thereof roar and be troubled, though the mountains shake
with the swelling thereof. Selah.

Psalms 146:7 Though I walk in the midst of trouble, thou wilt revive me: thou shalt stretch forth thine hand against the wrath of mine enemies, and thy right hand shall save me.

Psalms 18:2 The LORD is my rock, and my fortress, and my deliverer; my God, my strength, in whom I will trust; my buckler, and the horn of my salvation, and my high tower.

Psalms 22:24 For he hath not despised nor abhorred the affliction of the afflicted; neither hath he hid his face from him; but when he cried unto him, he heard.

Psalms 37:24 Though he fall, he shall not be utterly cast down: for the LORD upholdeth him with his hand.

Nahum 1:7 The LORD is good, a strong hold in the day of trouble; and he knoweth them that trust in him.

Psalms 37:39 But the salvation of the righteous is of the LORD: he is their strength in the time of trouble.

Psalms 55:22 Cast thy burden upon the LORD, and he shall sustain thee: he shall never suffer the righteous to be moved.

John 16:33 These things I have spoken unto you, that in me ye might have peace. In the world ye shall have tribulation: but be of good cheer; I have overcome the world.

Matthew 11:28 Come unto me, all ye that labour and are heavy laden, and I will give you rest.

2 Corinthians 1:5 For as the sufferings of Christ abound in us, so our consolation also aboundeth by Christ.

Psalms 9:9 The LORD also will be a refuge for the oppressed, a refuge in times of trouble.

Lamentations 3:31-33
For the Lord will not cast off for ever: 32 But though he cause grief, yet will he have compassion according to the multitude of his mercies. 33 For he doth not afflict willingly nor grieve the children of men.

Psalms 27:14 Wait on the LORD: be of good courage, and he shall strengthen thine heart: wait, I say, on the LORD.

Psalms 34:15 The eyes of the LORD are upon the righteous, and his ears are open unto their cry.

Psalms 34:18 The LORD is nigh unto them that are of a broken heart; and saveth such as be of a contrite spirit.

Psalms 34:19 Many are the afflictions of the righteous: but the LORD delivereth him out of them all.

Psalms 55:22 God shall hear, and afflict them, even he that abideth of old. Selah. Because they have no changes, therefore they fear not God.

Psalms 94:19 In the multitude of my thoughts within me thy comforts delight my soul.
Isaiah 57:19 I have seen his ways, and will heal him: I will lead him also, and restore comforts unto him and to his mourners.

Isaiah 66:13a "As one whom his mother comforteth, so will I comfort you...?"

Jeremiah 31:13 Then shall the virgin rejoice in the dance, both young men and old together: for I will turn their mourning into joy, and will comfort them, and make them rejoice from their sorrow.

2 Corinthians 1:4-5 Who comforteth us in all our tribulation, that we may be able to comfort them which are in any trouble, by the comfort wherewith we ourselves are comforted of God. 5 For as the sufferings of Christ abound in us, so our consolation also aboundeth by Christ.

2 Thessalonians 2:16 Now our Lord Jesus Christ himself, and God, even our Father, which hath loved us, and hath given us everlasting consolation and good hope through grace.

2 Thessalonians 2:17 Comfort your hearts, and stablish you in every good word and work.

Contentment

1 Timothy 6:6 But godliness with contentment is great gain.

1 Timothy 6:7-10
For we brought nothing into this world, and it is certain we can carry nothing out. 8 And having food and raiment let us be therewith content. 9 But they that will be rich fall into temptation and a snare, and into many foolish and hurtful lusts, which drown men in destruction and perdition. 10 For the love of money is the root of all evil: which while some coveted after, they have erred from the faith, and pierced themselves through with many sorrows.

Hebrews 13:5 Let your conversation be without covetousness; and be content with such things as ye have: for he hath said, I will never leave thee, nor forsake thee.

Deuteronomy 31:6 Be strong and of a good courage, fear not, nor be afraid of them: for the LORD thy God, he it is that doth go with thee; he will not fail thee, nor forsake thee.

Philippians 4:11-13
Not that I speak in respect of want: for I have learned, in whatsoever state I am, therewith to be content. 12 I know both how to be abased, and I know how to abound: every where and in all things I am instructed both to be full and to be hungry, both to abound and to suffer need. 12 I know both how to be abased, and I know how to abound: every where and in all things I am instructed both to be

full and to be hungry, both to abound and to suffer need. 13 I can do all things through Christ which strengtheneth me.

Proverbs 17:1 Better is a dry morsel, and quietness therewith, than an house full of sacrifices with strife.

Luke 12:15 And he said unto them, Take heed, and beware of covetousness: for a man's life consisteth not in the abundance of the things which he possesseth

Luke 12:16-21
And he spake a parable unto them, saying, the ground of a certain rich man brought forth plentifully: 17 And he thought within himself, saying, what shall I do, because I have no room where to bestow my fruits? 18 And he said, this will I do: I will pull down my barns, and build greater; and there will I bestow all my fruits and my goods. 19 And I will say to my soul, Soul, thou hast much goods laid up for many years; take thine ease, eat, drink, and be merry. 20 But God said unto him, Thou fool, this night thy soul shall be required of thee: then whose shall those things be, which thou hast provided? 21 So is he that layeth up treasure for himself, and is not rich toward God.

Mark 4:1-10; See also Mark 4:11-20
And he began again to teach by the sea side: and there was gathered unto him a great multitude, so that he entered into a ship, and sat in the sea; and the whole multitude was by the sea on the land. 2 And he taught them many things by parables, and said unto them in his doctrine, 3 Hearken; Behold, there went out a sower to sow: 4 And it came to pass, as he sowed, some fell by the way side, and the fowls of the air came and devoured it up. 5 And some fell on stony ground, where it had not much earth; and immediately it sprang up, because it had no depth of earth: 6 But when the sun was up, it was scorched; and because it had no root, it withered away. 7 And some fell among thorns, and the thorns grew up, and choked it, and it yielded no fruit. 8 And other fell on good ground, and did yield

fruit that sprang up and increased; and brought forth, some thirty, and some sixty, and some an hundred. 9 And he said unto them, He that hath ears to hear, let him hear. 10 And when he was alone, they that were about him with the twelve asked of him the parable..."

Mark 4:7 And some fell among thorns, and the thorns grew up, and choked it, and it yielded no fruit.

Mark 4:18-20
And these are they which are sown among thorns; such as hear the word, 19 And the cares of this world, and the deceitfulness of riches, and the lusts of other things entering in, choke the word, and it becometh unfruitful. 20 And these are they which are sown on good ground; such as hear the word, and receive it, and bring forth fruit, some thirtyfold, some sixty, and some an hundred.

Colossians 3:5 Mortify therefore your members which are upon the earth; fornication, uncleanness, inordinate affection, evil concupiscence, and covetousness, which is idolatry:

Matthew 6:19-21
Lay not up for yourselves treasures upon earth, where moth and rust doth corrupt, and where thieves break through and steal: 20 But lay up for yourselves treasures in heaven, where neither moth nor rust doth corrupt, and where thieves do not break through nor steal: 21 For where your treasure is, there will your heart be also.

Matthew 6:24 No man can serve two masters: for either he will hate the one, and love the other; or else he will hold to the one, and despise the other. Ye cannot serve God and mammon.

Matthew 6:33 But seek ye first the kingdom of God, and his righteousness; and all these things shall be added unto you.

Luke 9:46-48 Then there arose a reasoning among them, which of them should be greatest. 47 And Jesus, perceiving the thought of their heart, took a child, and set him by him, 48 And said unto them, Whosoever shall receive this child in my name receiveth me: and whosoever shall receive me receiveth him that sent me: for he that is least among you all, the same shall be great.

Proverbs 15:16-17 Better is little with the fear of the LORD than great treasure and trouble therewith. 17 Better is a dinner of herbs where love is, than a stalled ox and hatred therewith.

Proverbs 17:1 Better is a dry morsel, and quietness therewith, than an house full of sacrifices with strife.

Proverbs 23:4-5 Labour not to be rich: cease from thine own wisdom. 5 Wilt thou set thine eyes upon that which is not? For riches certainly make themselves wings; they fly away as an eagle toward heaven.

Proverbs 28:6 Better is the poor that walketh in his uprightness, than he that is perverse in his ways, though he be rich.

Ecclesiastes 4:6 Better is an handful with quietness, than both the hands full with travail and vexation of spirit.

Proverbs 30:8-9 Remove far from me vanity and lies: give me neither poverty nor riches; feed me with food convenient for me: 9 Lest I be full, and deny thee, and say, who is the LORD? Or lest I be poor, and steal, and take the name of my God in vain.

Proverbs 16:16-17 How much better is it to get wisdom than gold! And to get understanding rather to be chosen than silver! 17 The highway of the upright is to depart from evil: he that keepeth his way preserveth his soul.

Proverbs 22:1 A good name is rather to be chosen than great riches, and loving favour Contentment rather than silver and gold.

1 Kings 21:1-14

And it came to pass after these things, that Naboth the Jezreelite had a vineyard, which was in Jezreel, hard by the palace of Ahab king of Samaria. 2 And Ahab spake unto Naboth, saying, Give me thy vineyard, that I may have it for a garden of herbs, because it is near unto my house: and I will give thee for it a better vineyard than it; or, if it seem good to thee, I will give thee the worth of it in money. 3 And Naboth said to Ahab, The LORD forbid it me, that I should give the inheritance of my fathers unto thee. 4 And Ahab came into his house heavy and displeased because of the word which Naboth the Jezreelite had spoken to him: for he had said, I will not give thee the inheritance of my fathers. And he laid him down upon his bed, and turned away his face, and would eat no bread. 5 But Jezebel his wife came to him, and said unto him, why is thy spirit so sad, that thou eatest no bread? 6 And he said unto her, because I spake unto Naboth the Jezreelite, and said unto him, give me thy vineyard for money; or else, if it please thee, I will give thee another vineyard for it: and he answered, I will not give thee my vineyard. 7 And Jezebel his wife said unto him, Dost thou now govern the kingdom of Israel? Arise, and eat bread, and let thine heart be merry: I will give thee the vineyard of Naboth the Jezreelite. 8 So she wrote letters in Ahab's name, and sealed them with his seal, and sent the letters unto the elders and to the nobles that were in his city, dwelling with Naboth. :9 And she wrote in the letters, saying, Proclaim a fast, and set Naboth on high among the people: 10 And set two men, sons of Belial, before him, to bear witness against him, saying, Thou didst blaspheme God and the king. And then carry him out, and stone him, that he may die. 11 And the men of his city, even the elders and the nobles who were the inhabitants in his city, did as Jezebel had sent unto them, and as it was written in the letters which she had sent unto them. 12 They proclaimed a fast, and set Naboth on high among the people. 13 And there came in two men, children of Belial, and sat before him: and the men of Belial witnessed against him, even against Naboth, in the presence of the people, saying, Naboth did blaspheme God and the king. Then they carried him forth out of the city, and stoned him with stones, that he died. 14 Then they sent to Jezebel, saying, Naboth is stoned, and is dead.

1 Kings 21:2-4
And Ahab spake unto Naboth, saying, Give me thy vineyard, that I may have it for a garden of herbs, because it is near unto my house: and I will give thee for it a better vineyard than it; or, if it seem good to thee, I will give thee the worth of it in money.3 And Naboth said to Ahab, The LORD forbid it me, that I should give the inheritance of my fathers unto thee. 4 And Ahab came into his house heavy and displeased because of the word which Naboth the Jezreelite had spoken to him: for he had said, I will not give thee the inheritance of my fathers. And he laid him down upon his bed, and turned away his face, and would eat no bread.

2 Kings 20:12-19
At that time Berodachbaladan, the son of Baladan, king of Babylon, sent letters and a present unto Hezekiah: for he had heard that Hezekiah had been sick. 13 And Hezekiah hearkened unto them, and showed them all the house of his precious things, the silver, and the gold, and the spices, and the precious ointment, and all the house of his armour, and all that was found in his treasures: there was nothing in his house, nor in all his dominion, that Hezekiah showed them not. 14 Then came Isaiah the prophet unto King Hezekiah, and said unto him, what said these men? And from whence came they unto thee? And Hezekiah said, they are come from a far country, even from Babylon. 15 And he said, what have they seen in thine house? And Hezekiah answered, all the things that are in mine house have they seen: there is nothing among my treasures that I have not showed them. 16 And Isaiah said unto Hezekiah, Hear the word of the LORD. 17 Behold, the days come, that all that is in thine house, and that which thy fathers have laid up in store unto this day, shall be carried into Babylon: nothing shall be left, saith the LORD. 18 And of thy at that time Berodachbaladan, the son of Baladan, king of Babylon, sent letters and a present unto Hezekiah: for he had heard that Hezekiah had been sick. 13 And

Hezekiah hearkened unto them, and showed them all the house of his precious things, the silver, and the gold, and the spices, and the precious ointment, and all the house of his armour, and all that was found in his treasures: there was nothing in his house, nor in all his dominion, that Hezekiah showed them not. 14 Then came Isaiah the prophet unto king Hezekiah, and said unto him, What said these men? And from whence came they unto thee? And Hezekiah said, they are come from a far country, even from Babylon. 15 And he said, what have they seen in thine house? And Hezekiah answered, All the things that are in mine house have they seen: there is nothing among my treasures that I have not showed them. 16 And Isaiah said unto Hezekiah, Hear the word of the LORD. 17 Behold, the days come, that all that is in thine house, and that which thy fathers have laid up in store unto this day, shall be carried into Babylon: nothing shall be left, saith the LORD. 18 And of thy sons that shall issue from thee, which thou shalt beget, shall they take away; and they shall be eunuchs in the palace of the king of Babylon. 19 Then said Hezekiah unto Isaiah, Good is the word of the LORD which thou hast spoken. And he said, Is it not good, if peace and truth be in my days? 20 And the rest of the acts of Hezekiah, and all his might, and how he made a pool, and a conduit, and brought water into the city, are they not written in the book of the chronicles of the kings of Judah?

2 Kings 20:14-19
Then came Isaiah the prophet unto King Hezekiah, and said unto him, what said these men? And from whence came they unto thee? And Hezekiah said, they are come from a far country, even from Babylon. 15 And he said, what have they seen in thine house? And Hezekiah answered, all the things that are in mine house have they seen: there is nothing among my treasures that I have not showed them. 16 And Isaiah said unto Hezekiah, Hear the word of the LORD. 17 Behold, the days come, that all that is in thine house, and that which thy fathers have laid up in store unto this day, shall be carried into Babylon: nothing shall be left, saith the LORD. 18 And of thy sons that shall issue from thee, which thou shalt beget,

shall they take away; and they shall be eunuchs in the palace of the king of Babylon. 19 Then said Hezekiah unto Isaiah, Good is the word of the LORD which thou hast spoken. And he said, is it not good, if peace and truth be in my days?

Hebrews 3:17-19
Although the fig tree shall not blossom, neither shall fruit be in the vines; the labour of the olive shall fail, and the fields shall yield no meat; the flock shall be cut off from the fold, and there shall be no herd in the stalls: 18 Yet I will rejoice in the LORD, I will joy in the God of my salvation. 19 The LORD God is my strength, and he will make my feet like hinds' feet, and he will make me to walk upon mine high places. To the chief singer on my stringed instruments.

2 Kings 5:19-27
And he said unto him, Go in peace. So he departed from him a little way. 20 But Gehazi, the servant of Elisha the man of God, said, Behold, my master hath spared Naaman this Syrian, in not receiving at his hands that which he brought: but, as the LORD liveth, I will run after him, and take somewhat of him. 21 So Gehazi followed after Naaman. And when Naaman saw him running after him, he lighted down from the chariot to meet him, and said, Is all well? 22 And he said, All is well. My master hath sent me, saying, Behold, even now there be come to me from mount Ephraim two young men of the sons of the prophets: give them, I pray thee, a talent of silver, and two changes of garments. 23 And Naaman said, Be content, take two talents. And he urged him, and bound two talents of silver in two bags, with two changes of garments, and laid them upon two of his servants; and they bare them before him. 24 And when he came to the tower, he took them from their hand, and bestowed them in the house: and he let the men go, and they departed. 25 But he went in, and stood before his master. And Elisha said unto him, Whence comest thou, Gehazi? And he said, Thy servant went no whither. 26 And he said unto him, Went not mine heart with thee, when the man turned again from his chariot to meet thee? Is it a time to receive money, and to receive garments, and oliveyards, and

vineyards, and sheep, and oxen, and menservants, and maidservants? 27 The leprosy therefore of Naaman shall cleave unto thee, and unto thy seed for ever. And he went out from his presence a leper as white as snow.

2 Kings 5:19-20
And he said unto him, Go in peace. So he departed from him a little way. 20 But Gehazi, the servant of Elisha the man of God, said, Behold, my master hath spared Naaman this Syrian, in not receiving at his hands that which he brought: but, as the LORD liveth, I will run after him, and take somewhat of him.

2 Kings 5:27 The leprosy therefore of Naaman shall cleave unto thee, and unto thy seed for ever. And he went out from his presence a leper as white as snow.

Ecclesiastes 5:8-17
If thou seest the oppression of the poor, and violent perverting of judgment and justice in a province, marvel not at the matter: for he that is higher than the highest regardeth; and there be higher than they. 9 Moreover the profit of the earth is for all: the king himself is served by the field. 10 He that loveth silver shall not be satisfied with silver; nor he that loveth abundance with increase: this is also vanity. 11 When goods increase, they are increased that eat them: and what good is there to the owners thereof, saving the beholding of them with their eyes? The sleep of a labouring man is sweet, whether he eat little or much: but the abundance of the rich will not suffer him to sleep. 13 There is a sore evil which I have seen under the sun, namely, riches kept for the owners thereof to their hurt. 14 But those riches perish by evil travail: and he begetteth a son, and there is nothing in his hand. 15 As he came forth of his mother's womb, naked shall he return to go as he came, and shall take nothing of his labour, which he may carry away in his hand. 16 And this also is a sore evil, that in all points as he came, so shall he go: and what profit hath he that hath labouredly for the wind? 17 All his days also he eateth in darkness, and he hath much sorrow and wrath with his sickness.

Ecclesiastes 5:10-11
He that loveth silver shall not be satisfied with silver; nor he that loveth abundance with increase: this is also vanity. 11 When goods increase, they are increased that eat them: and what good is there to the owners thereof, saving the beholding of them with their eyes?

Ecclesiastes 5:15-17
As he came forth of his mother's womb, naked shall he return to go as he came, and shall take nothing of his labour, which he may carry away in his hand. 16 And this also is a sore evil, that in all points as he came, so shall he go: and what profit hath he that hath laboured for the wind? 17 All his days also he eateth in darkness, and he hath much sorrow and wrath with his sickness.

Ecclesiastes 12:13-14
Let us hear the conclusion of the whole matter: Fear God, and keep his commandments: for this is the whole duty of man. 14 For God shall bring every work into judgment, with every secret thing, whether it be good, or whether it be evil.

Matthew 6:33 But seek ye first the kingdom of God, and his righteousness; and all these things shall be added unto you.

2 Corinthian 4:18 While we look not at the things which are seen, but at the things which are not seen: for the things which are seen are temporal; but the things which are not seen are eternal.

Colossians 3:1-3
If ye then be risen with Christ, seek those things which are above, where Christ sitteth on the right hand of God. 2 Set your affection on things above, not on things on the earth. 3 For ye are dead, and your life is hid with Christ in God.

Courage

Psalms 27:14 Wait on the LORD: be of good courage, and he shall strengthen thine heart: wait, I say, on the LORD.

Psalms 37:28 For the LORD loveth judgment, and forsaketh not his saints; they are preserved for ever: but the seed of the wicked shall be cut off.

Isaiah 43:1 But now thus saith the LORD that created thee, O Jacob, and he that formed thee, O Israel, Fear not: for I have redeemed thee, I have called thee by thy name; thou art mine.

2 Kings 6:16 And he answered, Fear not: for they that be with us are more than they that be with them

Psalms 37:3 Trust in the LORD, and do good; so shalt thou dwell in the land, and verily thou shalt be fed.

Isaiah 40:29 He giveth power to the faint; and to them that have no might he increaseth strength.

Psalms 31:24 Be of good courage, and he shall strengthen your heart, all ye that hope in the LORD.

Philippians 4:12-13
Know both how to be abased, and I know how to abound: every where and in all things I am instructed both to be full and to be hungry, both to abound and to suffer need. 13 I can do all things through Christ which strengtheneth me.

Death

Psalms 23:4 Yea, though I walk through the valley of the shadow of death, I will fear no evil: for thou art with me; thy rod and thy staff they comfort me

Psalms 23:6 Surely goodness and mercy shall follow me all the days of my life: and I will dwell in the house of the LORD for ever.

Psalms 116:15 Precious in the sight of the LORD is the death of his saints.

Proverbs 14:32 The wicked is driven away in his wickedness: but the righteous hath hope in his death.

John 5:21 For as the Father raiseth up the dead, and quickeneth them; even so the Son quickeneth whom he will.

John 5:24 Verily, verily, I say unto you, He that heareth my word, and believeth on him that sent me, hath everlasting life, and shall not come into condemnation; but is passed from death unto life.

John 5:28 Marvel not at this: for the hour is coming, in the which all that are in the graves shall hear his voice,

John 11:25-26 Jesus said unto her, I am the resurrection, and the life: he that believeth in me, though he were dead, yet shall he live: 26

And whosoever liveth and believeth in me shall never die. Believest thou this?

1 Corinthians 15:53-54
For this corruptible must put on incorruption, and this mortal must put on immortality. 54 So when this corruptible shall have put on incorruption, and this mortal shall have put on immortality, then shall be brought to pass the saying that is written, Death is swallowed up in victory.

1 Corinthians 15:56-57 O death, where is thy sting? O grave, where is thy victory? 56 The sting of death is sin; and the strength of sin is the law. 57 But thanks be to God, which giveth us the victory through our Lord Jesus Christ.

2 Corinthians 5:8 We are confident, I say, and willing rather to be absent from the body, and to be present with the Lord.

Hebrews 9:27 And as it is appointed unto men once to die, but after this the judgment:

Philippians 1:21 For to me to live is Christ, and to die is gain.

Hebrews 2:14 Forasmuch then as the children are partakers of flesh and blood, he also himself likewise took part of the same; that through death he might destroy him that had the power of death, that is, the devil.

Hebrews 2:15 And deliver them who through fear of death were all their lifetime subject to bondage.

Proverbs 14:32 The wicked is driven away in his wickedness: but the righteous hath hope in his death.

Romans 5:9 Much more then, being now justified by his blood, we shall be saved from wrath through him.

Hebrews 2:14-15
Forasmuch then as the children are partakers of flesh and blood, he also himself likewise took part of the same; that through death he might destroy him that had the power of death, that is, the devil; 15 And deliver them who through fear of death were all their lifetime subject to bondage.
John 8:51 Verily, verily, I say unto you, if a man keep my saying, he shall never see death.

Psalms 48:14 For this God is our God for ever and ever: he will be our guide even unto death.

Psalms 73:26 My flesh and my heart faileth: but God is the strength of my heart, and my portion for ever.

Psalms 49:15 But God will redeem my soul from the power of the grave: for he shall receive me. Selah.

Isaiah 25:8 He will swallow up death in victory; and the Lord GOD will wipe away tears from off all faces; and the rebuke of his people shall he take away from off all the earth: for the LORD hath spoken it.

Hosea 13:14 I will ransom them from the power of the grave; I will redeem them from death: O death, I will be thy plagues; O grave, I will be thy destruction: repentance shall be hid from mine eyes.

Psalms 37:37 Mark the perfect man, and behold the upright: for the end of that man is peace.

2 Corinthians 4:16 For which cause we faint not; but though our outward man perish, yet the inward man is renewed day by day.

John 3:15 That whosoever believeth in him should not perish, but have eternal life.

Romans 8:38-39
For I am persuaded, that neither death, nor life, nor angels, nor
principalities, nor powers, nor things present, nor things to come,
39 Nor height, nor depth, nor any other creature, shall be able
to separate us from the love of God, which is in Christ Jesus our
Lord.

Eternal life

John 6:47 Verily, verily, I say unto you, He that believeth on me hath everlasting life.

John 11:25-26 Jesus said unto her, I am the resurrection, and the life: he that believeth in me, though he were dead, yet shall he live: 26 And whosoever liveth and believeth in me shall never die. Believest thou this?

1 Corinthians 15:51-54
Behold, I show you a mystery; we shall not all sleep, but we shall all be changed, 52 In a moment, in the twinkling of an eye, at the last trump: for the trumpet shall sound, and the dead shall be raised incorruptible, and we shall be changed. 53 For this corruptible must put on incorruption, and this mortal must put on immortality. 54 So when this corruptible shall have put on incorruption, and this mortal shall have put on immortality, then shall be brought to pass the saying that is written, Death is swallowed up in victory.

1 John 2:25 And this is the promise that he hath promised us, even eternal life.

1 Corinthians 15:21 For since by man came death, by man came also the resurrection of the dead.

1 John 5:13
These things have I written unto you that believe on the name of the Son of God; that ye may know that ye have eternal life, and that ye may believe on the name of the Son of God.

John 5:28-29
Marvel not at this: for the hour is coming, in the which all that are in the graves shall hear his voice, 29 And shall come forth; they that have done good, unto the resurrection of life; and they that have done evil, unto the resurrection of damnation.

1 Thessalonians 4:16
That no man go beyond and defraud his brother in any matter: because that the Lord is the avenger of all such, as we also have forewarned you and testified.

Revelation 7:15-17
Therefore are they before the throne of God, and serve him day and night in his temple: and he that sitteth on the throne shall dwell among them. 16 They shall hunger no more, neither thirst any more; neither shall the sun light on them, nor any heat. 17 For the Lamb which is in the midst of the throne shall feed them, and shall lead them unto living fountains of waters: and God shall wipe away all tears from their eyes.

John 3:16
For God so loved the world, that he gave his only begotten Son, that whosoever believeth in him should not perish, but have everlasting life.

1 Corinthians 15:42-46
So also is the resurrection of the dead. It is sown in corruption; it is raised in incorruption: 43 It is sown in dishonour; it is raised in glory: it is sown in weakness; it is raised in power: 44 It is sown a natural body; it is raised a spiritual body. There is a natural body, and

there is a spiritual body. 45 And so it is written, The first man Adam was made a living soul; the last Adam was made a quickening spirit. 46 Howbeit that was not first which is spiritual, but that which is natural; and afterward that which is spiritual.

Romans 8:11
But if the Spirit of him that raised up Jesus from the dead dwell in you, he that raised up Christ from the dead shall also quicken your mortal bodies by his Spirit that dwelleth in you.

Revelation 21:4 And God shall wipe away all tears from their eyes; and there shall be no more death, neither sorrow, nor crying, neither shall there be any more pain: for the former things are passed away.

Romans 6:23 For the wages of sin is death; but the gift of God is eternal life through Jesus Christ our Lord.

Job 19:26-27 And though after my skin worms destroy this body, yet in my flesh shall I see God: 27 Whom I shall see for myself, and mine eyes shall behold, and not another; though my reins be consumed within me.

Galatians 6:8 For he that soweth to his flesh shall of the flesh reap corruption; but he that soweth to the Spirit shall of the Spirit reap life everlasting.

Daniel 12:2 And many of them that sleep in the dust of the earth shall awake, some to everlasting life, and some to shame and everlasting contempt.

Isaiah 26:19 Thy dead men shall live; together with my dead body shall they arise. Awake and sing, ye that dwell in dust: for thy dew is as the dew of herbs, and the earth shall cast out the dead.

Psalms 16:10 For thou wilt not leave my soul in hell; neither wilt thou suffer thine Holy One to see corruption.

2 Timothy 1:10 But is now made manifest by the appearing of our Saviour Jesus Christ, who hath abolished death, and hath brought life and immortality to light through the gospel:

1 John 5:11 And this is the record, that God hath given to us eternal life, and this life is in his Son.

2 Corinthians 5:1 For we know that if our earthly house of this tabernacle were dissolved, we have a building of God, an house not made with hands, eternal in the heavens.

John 14:2-3
In my Father's house are many mansions: if it were not so, I would have told you. I go to prepare a place for you. 3 And if I go and prepare a place for you, I will come again, and receive you unto myself; that where I am, there ye may be also.

John 6:39-40
This is the Father's will which hath sent me, that of all which he hath given me I should lose nothing, but should raise it up again at the last day. 40 And this is the will of him that sent me, that every one which seeth the Son, and believeth on him, may have everlasting life: and I will raise him up at the last day.

Luke 20:35-36
But they which shall be accounted worthy to obtain that world, and the resurrection from the dead, neither marry, nor are given in marriage: 36 Neither can they die any more: for they are equal unto the angels; and are the children of God, being the children of the resurrection.

John 10:27-28 My sheep hear my voice, and I know them, and they follow me: 28 And I give unto them eternal life; and they shall never perish, neither shall any man pluck them out of my hand.

John 6:54
Whoso eateth my flesh, and drinketh my blood, hath eternal life; and I will raise him up at the last day.

Faith

Hebrews 11:1 Now faith is the substance of things hoped for, the evidence of things not seen.

Matthew 9:29 "… According to your faith be it unto you."

Matthew 15:28b "… O woman, great is thy faith: be it unto thee even as thou wilt..."

Matthew 21:21 "… Verily I say unto you, if ye have faith, and doubt not, ye shall not only do this which is done to the fig tree, but also if ye shall say unto this mountain, be thou removed… it shall be done."

Romans 1:17 For therein is the righteousness of God revealed from faith to faith: as it is written, the just shall live by faith.

Romans 5:1 Therefore being justified by faith, we have peace with God through our Lord Jesus Christ:

Romans 10:8 But what saith it? The word is nigh thee, even in thy mouth, and in thy heart: that is, the word of faith, which we preach;

Romans 10:17 So then faith cometh by hearing, and hearing by the word of God.

Romans 12:3c "... God hath dealt to every man the measure of faith."

1 Corinthians 2:5 That your faith should not stand in the wisdom of men, but in the power of God.

Ephesians 2:8 For by grace are ye saved through faith; and that not of yourselves: it is the gift of God.

Philemon 1:6 That the communication of thy faith may become effectual by the acknowledging of every good thing which is in you in Christ Jesus.

Faithfulness, Gods

Deuteronomy 7:9 Know therefore that the LORD thy God, he is God, the faithful God, which keepeth covenant and mercy with them that love him and keep his commandments to a thousand generations

Deuteronomy 4:31 For the LORD thy God is a merciful God; he will not forsake thee, neither destroy thee, nor forget the covenant of thy fathers which he sware unto them.

Psalms 105:8 He hath remembered his covenant for ever, the word which he commanded to a thousand generations.

Numbers 23:19 God is not a man, that he should lie; neither the son of man, that he should repent: hath he said, and shall he not do it? Or hath he spoken, and shall he not make it good?

Hebrews 10:23 Let us hold fast the profession of our faith without wavering; (for he is faithful that promised ;)

2 Timothy 2:13 If we believe not, yet he abideth faithful: he cannot deny himself.

2 Peter 3:9 The Lord is not slack concerning his promise, as some men count slackness; but is longsuffering to us-ward, not willing that any should perish, but that all should come to repentance.

Kings 8:56 Blessed be the LORD, that hath given rest unto his people Israel, according to all that he promised: there hath not failed one word of all his good promise… "

Isaiah 25:1 O LORD, thou art my God; I will exalt thee, I will praise thy name; for thou hast done wonderful things; thy counsels of old are faithfulness and truth.

Psalms 9:10 And they that know thy name will put their trust in thee: for thou, LORD, hast not forsaken them that seek thee.

Psalms 119:160 Thy word is true from the beginning: and every one of thy righteous Faithfulness, Gods judgments endureth for ever.

Psalms119:89-90 LAMED. For ever, O LORD, thy word is settled in heaven. 90 Thy faithfulness is unto all generations: thou hast established the earth, and it abideth.

1 Samuel 15:29 And also the Strength of Israel will not lie nor repent: for he is not a man, that he should repent.

Psalms 89:34 My covenant will I not break, nor alter the thing that is gone out of my lips.

Isaiah 54:10 For the mountains shall depart, and the hills be removed; but my kindness shall not depart from thee, neither shall the covenant of my peace be removed, saith the LORD that hath mercy on thee.

Isaiah 46:11 Calling a ravenous bird from the east, the man that executeth my counsel from a far country: yea, I have spoken it, I will also bring it to pass; I have purposed it, I will also do it.

Fear

Luke 12:32 Fear not, little flock; for it is your Father's good pleasure to give you the kingdom.

Mark 4:40 And he said unto them, Why are ye so fearful? How is it that ye have no faith?

Matthew 10:28 And fear not them which kill the body, but are not able to kill the soul: but rather fear him which is able to destroy both soul and body in hell.

Isaiah 41:13 For I the LORD thy God will hold thy right hand, saying unto thee, Fear not; I will help thee.

Proverbs 1:33 But whoso hearkeneth unto me shall dwell safely, and shall be quiet from fear of evil.

Isaiah 43:2
When thou passest through the waters, I will be with thee; and through the rivers, they shall not overflow thee: when thou walkest through the fire, thou shalt not be burned; neither shall the flame kindle upon thee.

John 14:27 Peace I leave with you, my peace I give unto you: not as the world giveth, give I unto you. Let not your heart be troubled, neither let it be afraid.

Psalms 23:4-5 Yea, though I walk through the valley of the shadow of death, I will fear no evil: for thou art with me; thy rod and thy staff they comfort me. 5 Thou preparest a table before me in the presence of mine enemies: thou anointest my head with oil; my cup runneth over.

Psalms 27:1-3
A Psalm of David. The LORD is my light and my salvation; whom shall I fear? The LORD is the strength of my life; of whom shall I be afraid? 2 When the wicked, even mine enemies and my foes, came upon me to eat up my flesh, they stumbled and fell. 3 Though an host should encamp against me, my heart shall not fear: though war should rise against me, in this will I be confident.

Romans 8:37-39
Nay, in all these things we are more than conquerors through him that loved us. 38 For I am persuaded, that neither death, nor life, nor angels, nor principalities, nor powers, nor things present, nor things to come, 39 Nor height, nor depth, nor any other creature, shall be able to separate us from the love of God, which is in Christ Jesus our Lord.

Psalms 34:4 I sought the LORD, and he heard me, and delivered me from all my fears.

1 Peter 5:7 Casting all your care upon him; for he careth for you.

Philippians 4-8 Finally, brethren, whatsoever things are true, whatsoever things are honest, whatsoever things are just, whatsoever things are pure, whatsoever things are lovely, whatsoever things are of good report; if there be any virtue, and if there be any praise, think on these things.

Joshua 1:9 Have not I commanded thee? Be strong and of a good courage; be not afraid, neither be thou dismayed: for the LORD thy God is with thee whithersoever thou goest.

Isaiah 41:10 Fear thou not; for I am with thee: be not dismayed; for I am thy God: I will strengthen thee; yea, I will help thee; yea, I will uphold thee with the right hand of my righteousness.

Isaiah 41:13 For I the LORD thy God will hold thy right hand, saying unto thee, Fear not; I will help thee.

Psalms 73:23-24 Nevertheless I am continually with thee: thou hast holden me by my right hand. 24 Thou shalt guide me with thy counsel, and afterward receive me to glory.

1 John 4:18 There is no fear in love; but perfect love casteth out fear: because fear hath torment. He that feareth is not made perfect in love.

1 John 3:5-6 Trust in the LORD with all thine heart; and lean not unto thine own understanding. 6 In all thy ways acknowledge him, and he shall direct thy paths.

Matthew 6:34 Take therefore no thought for the morrow: for the morrow shall take thought for the things of itself. Sufficient unto the day is the evil thereof.

Matthew 6:26-33
Behold the fowls of the air: for they sow not, neither do they reap, nor gather into barns; yet your heavenly Father feedeth them. Are ye not much better than they? 27 Which of you by taking thought can add one cubit unto his stature? 28 And why take ye thought for raiment? Consider the lilies of the field, how they grow; they toil not, neither do they spin: 29 And yet I say unto you, That even Solomon in all his glory was not arrayed like one of these. 30 Wherefore, if God so clothe the grass of the field, which to day is, and to morrow is cast into the oven, shall he not much more clothe you, O ye of little faith? 31 Therefore take no thought, saying, What shall we eat? Or, what shall we drink? Or, Wherewithal shall we be clothed? 32 (For after all these things do the Gentiles seek:) for your heavenly

Father knoweth that ye have need of all these things. 33 But seek ye first the kingdom of God, and his righteousness; and all these things shall be added unto you.

Isaiah 43:18-19 Remember ye not the former things, neither consider the things of old. 19 Behold, I will do a new thing; now it shall spring forth; shall ye not know it? I will even make a way in the wilderness, and rivers in the desert.

Psalms 91:4 He shall cover thee with his feathers, and under his wings shalt thou trust: his truth shall be thy shield and buckler.

Food and Clothing

Joel 2:26 And ye shall eat in plenty, and be satisfied, and praise the name of the LORD your God, that hath dealt wondrously with you: and my people shall never be ashamed.

Psalms 147: 14 He maketh peace in thy borders, and filleth thee with the finest of the wheat.

Psalms 111:5 He hath given meat unto them that fear him: he will ever be mindful of his covenant.

Proverbs 13:25 The righteous eateth to the satisfying of his soul: but the belly of the wicked shall want.

Psalms 132:15 I will abundantly bless her provision: I will satisfy her poor with bread.

Matthew 6:31-32
Therefore take no thought, saying, what shall we eat? Or, what shall we drink? Or, Wherewithal shall we be clothed? 32 (For after all these things do the Gentiles seek :) for your heavenly Father knoweth that ye have need of all these things.

Forgiveness

Matthew 5:44-45
But I say unto you, Love your enemies, bless them that curse you, do
good to them that hate you, and pray for them which despitefully use
you, and persecute you; [45] That ye may be the children of your Father
which is in heaven: for he maketh his sun to rise on the evil and on
the good, and sendeth rain on the just and on the unjust.

Mark 11:25 And when ye stand praying, forgive, if ye have ought against any: that your Father also which is in heaven may forgive you your trespasses.

Mark 11:26 But if ye do not forgive, neither will your Father which is in heaven forgive your trespasses.

1 John 1:9 If we confess our sins, he is faithful and just to forgive us *our* sins, and to cleanse us from all unrighteousness

Matthew 6:14 For if ye forgive men their trespasses, your heavenly Father will also forgive you.

Matthew 6:15 But if ye forgive not men their trespasses, neither will your Father forgive your trespasses.

Romans 4:7 *Saying,* Blessed *are* they whose iniquities are forgiven, and whose sins are covered.

2 Corinthians 2:10 To whom ye forgive any thing, I *forgive* also: for if I forgave any thing, to whom I forgave *it,* for your sakes *forgave I it* in the person of Christ.

Ephesians 4:32 And be ye kind one to another, tenderhearted, forgiving one another even as God for Christ's sake hath forgiven you.

Romans 12:20 Therefore if thine enemy hunger, feed him; if he thirst, give him drink for in so doing thou shalt heap coals of fire on his head.

Luke 6:35-38
But love ye your enemies, and do good, and lend, hoping for nothing again; and your reward shall be great, and ye shall be the children of the Highest: for he is kind unto the unthankful and to the evil.
[36] Be ye therefore merciful, as your Father also is merciful. [37] Judge
not, and ye shall not be judged: condemn not, and ye shall not be
condemned forgive, and ye shall be forgiven: [38] Give, and it shall be
given unto you good measure, pressed down, and shaken together, and running over shall men give into your bosom. For with the same measure that ye mete withal it shall be measured to you again.

Proverbs 20:22 Say not thou, I will recompense evil; *but* wait on the LORD, and he shall save thee.

Matthew 12:31 Wherefore I say unto you, All manner of sin and blasphemy shall bf forgiven unto men: but the blasphemy *against* the *Holy* Ghost shall no be forgiven unto men.

Matthew 12:32
And whosoever speaketh a word against the Son of man, it shall be forgiven him: but whosoever speaketh against the Holy Ghost, it shall not be forgiven him, neither in this world, neither in the *world* to come.

Matthew 18:21-22
Then came Peter to him, and said, Lord, how oft shall my brother sin against me, and 1 forgive him? Till seven times? [22] Jesus saith unto him, say not unto thee, until seven times: but, until seventy times seven.

Matthew 18:35 So likewise shall my heavenly Father do also unto you, if ye from your hearts forgive not every one his brother their trespasses.

Luke 5:24 But that ye may know that the Son of man hath power upon earth to forgive sins, (he said unto the sick of the palsy,) I say unto thee, Arise, and take up thy couch, and go into thine house.

Luke 6:37 Judge not, and ye shall not be judged: condemn not, and ye shall not be condemned: forgive, and ye shall be forgiven:

Luke 11:4 And forgive us our sins; for we also forgive every one that is indebted to us. And lead us not into temptation; but deliver us from evil.

Luke 17:3 Take heed to yourselves: If thy brother trespass against thee, rebuke him; and if he repent, forgive him.

Luke 17:4 And if he trespass against thee seven times in a day, and even times in a day turn again to thee, saying, I repent; thou shalt forgive him.

Luke 23:34 Then said Jesus, Father, forgive them; for they know not what they do. And they parted his raiment, and cast lots.

Acts 5:31 Him hath God exalted with his right hand *to be* a Prince and a Saviour, for to give repentance to Israel, and forgiveness of sins.

Acts 8:22 Repent therefore of this thy wickedness, and pray God, if perhaps the thought of thine heart may be forgiven thee.

Acts 13:38 Be it known unto you therefore, men *and* brethren, that through this man is preached unto you the forgiveness of sins:

Acts 26:18
To open their eyes, *and* to turn *them* from darkness to light, and *from* the power of Satan unto God, that they may receive forgiveness of sins and inheritance among them which are sanctified by faith that is in me.

Ephesians 1:7 In whom we have redemption through his blood, the forgiveness of sins, according to the riches of his grace.

Colossians 2:13 And you, being dead in your sins and the uncircumcision of your flesh hath he quickened together with him, having forgiven you al trespasses.

James 5:15 And the prayer of faith shall save the sick, and the Lord shall raise him up; and if he have committed sins, they shall be forgiven him.

1 John 2:12 I write unto you, little children, because your sins are forgiven you for his name's sake.

Fruitfulness

John 15:1-5
I am the true vine, and my Father is the husbandman.2 Every branch
in me that beareth not fruit he taketh away: and every branch that
beareth fruit, he purgeth it, that it may bring forth more fruit. 3
Now ye are clean through the word which I have spoken unto you.
4 Abide in me, and I in you. As the branch cannot bear fruit of itself,
except it abide in the vine; no more can ye, except ye abide in me.
5 I am the vine, ye are the branches: He that abideth in me, and I
in him, the same bringeth forth much fruit: for without me ye can
do nothing.

Psalms 1:3 And he shall be like a tree planted by the rivers of water, that bringeth forth his fruit in his season; his leaf also shall not wither; and whatsoever he doeth shall prosper.

Jeremiah 31:12
Therefore they shall come and sing in the height of Zion, and shall flow together to the goodness of the LORD, for wheat, and for wine, and for oil, and for the young of the flock and of the herd: and their soul shall be as a watered garden; and they shall not sorrow any more at all.

Psalms 92:14 They shall still bring forth fruit in old age; they shall be fat and flourishing.

Hosea 14:5 I will be as the dew unto Israel: he shall grow as the lily, and cast forth his roots as Lebanon.

2 Peter 1:8 For if these things be in you, and abound, they make you that ye shall neither be barren nor unfruitful in the knowledge of our Lord Jesus Christ.

Grace, Growing In

John 15:8 Herein is my Father glorified, that ye bear much fruit; so shall ye be my disciples.

Philippians 1:9 And this I pray, that your love may abound yet more and more in knowledge and in all judgment.

2 Thessalonians 1:3 We are bound to thank God always for you, brethren, as it is meet, because that your faith groweth exceedingly, and the charity of every one of you all toward each other aboundeth;

1Thessalonians 4:1 Furthermore then we beseech you, brethren, and exhort you by the Lord Jesus, that as ye have received of us how ye ought to walk and to please God, so ye would abound more and more.

Philippians 1:11 Being filled with the fruits of righteousness, which are by Jesus Christ, unto the glory and praise of God.

2 Peter 1:5 And beside this, giving all diligence, add to your faith virtue; and to virtue knowledge.

Job 17:9 The righteous also shall hold on his way, and he that hath clean hands shall be stronger and stronger.

2 Corinthians 3:18 But we all, with open face beholding as in a glass the glory of the Lord, are changed into the same image from glory to glory, even as by the Spirit of the Lord.

Psalms 138:8 The LORD will perfect that which concerneth me: thy mercy, O LORD, endureth for ever: forsake not the works of thine own hands.

Colossians 1:6 Which is come unto you, as it is in all the world; and bringeth forth fruit, as it doth also in you, since the day ye heard of it, and knew the grace of God in truth.

Philippians 3:14:16
I press toward the mark for the prize of the high calling of God in Grace, Christ Jesus. 15 Let us therefore, as many as be perfect, be thus minded: and if in any thing ye be otherwise minded, God shall reveal even this unto you. 16 Nevertheless, whereto we have already attained, let us walk by the same rule, let us mind the same thing.

Proverbs 4:18 But the path of the just is as the shining light, that shineth more and more unto the perfect day.

Guidance

Isaiah 30:21 And thine ears shall hear a word behind thee, saying, this is the way, walk ye in it, when ye turn to the right hand, and when ye turn to the left.

Psalms 48:14 For this God is our God for ever and ever: he will be our guide even unto death.

Proverbs 16:9 A man's heart deviseth his way: but the LORD directeth his steps.

Psalms 37:23 The steps of a good man are ordered by the LORD: and he delighteth in his way.

Isaiah 28:26 For his God doth instruct him to discretion, and doth teach him.

Proverbs 11:5 The righteousness of the perfect shall direct his way: but the wicked shall fall by his own wickedness.

Proverbs 3:6 In all thy ways acknowledge him, and he shall direct thy paths.

Psalms 32:8 I will instruct thee and teach thee in the way which thou shalt go: I will guide thee with mine eye.

Isaiah 42:16

And I will bring the blind by a way that they knew not; I will lead them in paths that they have not known: I will make darkness light before them, and crooked things straight. These things will I do unto them, and not forsake them.

Psalms 73:23-24 Nevertheless I am continually with thee: thou hast holden me by my right hand. 24 Thou shalt guide me with thy counsel, and afterward receive me to glory.

Guilt

1 John 1:9 If we confess our sins, he is faithful and just to forgive us our sins, and to cleanse us from all unrighteousness.

Isaiah 55:7 Let the wicked forsake his way, and the unrighteous man his thoughts: and let him return unto the LORD, and he will have mercy upon him; and to our God, for he will abundantly pardon.

2 Chronicles 30:9
For if ye turn again unto the LORD, your brethren and your children shall find compassion before them that lead them captive, so that they shall come again into this land: for the LORD your God is gracious and merciful, and will not turn away his face from you, if ye return unto him.

Psalms 103:12 As far as the east is from the west, so far hath he removed our transgressions from us.

1 John 3:20 For if our heart condemn us, God is greater than our heart, and knoweth all things.

Hebrews 8:12 For I will be merciful to their unrighteousness, and their sins and their iniquities will I remember no more.

2 Corinthians 5:17 Therefore if any man be in Christ, he is a new creature: old things are passed away; behold, all things are become new.

Jeremiah 31:34 And they shall teach no more every man his neighbour, and every man his brother, saying, Know the LORD: for they shall all know me, from the least of them unto the greatest of them, saith the LORD: for I will forgive their iniquity, and I will remember their sin no more.

Jeremiah 33:8 And I will cleanse them from all their iniquity, whereby they have sinned against me; and I will pardon all their iniquities, whereby they have sinned, and whereby they have transgressed against me.

1 John 2:12 I write unto you, little children, because your sins are forgiven you for his name's sake.

Isaiah 43:25 I, even I, am he that blotteth out thy transgressions for mine own sake, and will not remember thy sins.

1 John 1:7 But if we walk in the light, as he is in the light, we have fellowship one with another, and the blood of Jesus Christ his Son cleanseth us from all sin.

Healing

2 Chronicles 7:14
If my people, which are called by my name, shall humble themselves, and pray, and seek my face, and turn from their wicked ways; then will I hear from heaven, and will forgive their sin, and will heal their land.

Psalms 41:4 I said, LORD, be merciful unto me: heal my soul; for I have sinned against thee.

Ecclesiastes 3:3 A time to kill, and a time to heal; a time to break down, and a time to build up;

Jeremiah 3:22 Return, ye backsliding children, and I will heal your backslidings. Behold, we come unto thee; for thou art the LORD our God.

Malachi 4:2 But unto you that fear my name shall the Sun of righteousness arise with healing in his wings; and ye shall go forth, and grow up as calves of the stall.

Matthew 4:23
And Jesus went about all Galilee, teaching in their synagogues, and preaching the gospel of the kingdom, and healing all manner of sickness and all manner of disease among the people.

Matthew 10:8 Heal the sick, cleanse the lepers, raise the dead, cast out devils: freely ye have received, freely give.

Luke 4:18
The Spirit of the Lord is upon me, because he hath anointed me to preach the gospel to the poor; he hath sent me to heal the brokenhearted, to preach deliverance to the captives, and recovering of sight to the blind, to set at liberty them that are bruised,

Luke 9:2 And he sent them to preach the kingdom of God, and to heal the sick.

1 Corinthians12:30 Have all the gifts of healing? Do all speak with tongues? Do all interpret?

Help In Troubles

Psalms 37:39 But the salvation of the righteous is of the LORD: he is their strength in the time of trouble.

Psalms 146:8 The LORD openeth the eyes of the blind: the LORD raiseth them that are bowed down: the LORD loveth the righteous.

Nahum 1:7 The LORD is good, a strong hold in the day of trouble; and he knoweth them that trust in him.

Psalms 37:24 Though he fall, he shall not be utterly cast down: for the LORD upholdeth him with his hand.

Psalms 32:7 Thou art my hiding place; thou shalt preserve me from trouble; thou shalt compass me about with songs of deliverance. Selah.

Psalms 71:20 Thou, which hast showed me great and sore troubles, shalt quicken me again, and shalt bring me up again from the depths of the earth.

Psalms 42:11 Why art thou cast down, O my soul? And why art thou disquieted within me? Hope thou in God: for I shall yet praise him, who is the health of my countenance, and my God.

Psalms 73:26 My flesh and my heart faileth: but God is the strength of my heart, and my portion for ever.

Psalms 91:10-11 There shall no evil befall thee, neither shall any plague come nigh thy dwelling. 11 For he shall give his angels charge over thee, to keep thee in all thy ways.

Psalms 126:5-6 They that sow in tears shall reap in joy. 6 He that goeth forth and weepeth, bearing precious seed, shall doubtless come again with rejoicing, bringing his sheaves with him.

Psalms 31:23 O love the LORD, all ye his saints: for the LORD preserveth the faithful, and plentifully rewardeth the proud doer.

Psalms 68:13 Though ye have lien among the pots, yet shall ye be as the wings of a dove covered with silver, and her feathers with yellow gold.

Job 8:20-21 Behold, God will not cast away a perfect man, neither will he help the evil doers: 21 Till he fill thy mouth with laughing, and thy lips with rejoicing.

Job 5:19 He shall deliver thee in six troubles: yea, in seven there shall no evil touch thee.

Psalms 22-24 For he hath not despised nor abhorred the affliction of the afflicted; neither hath he hid his face from him; but when he cried unto him, he heard.

Psalms 9:9 The LORD also will be a refuge for the oppressed, a refuge in times of trouble.

Psalms 138:7 Though I walk in the midst of trouble, thou wilt revive me: thou shalt stretch forth thine hand against the wrath of mine enemies, and thy right hand shall save me.

Psalms 18:28 For thou wilt light my candle: the LORD my God will enlighten my darkness.

Psalms34:19 Many are the afflictions of the righteous: but the LORD delivereth him out of them all.

Lamentations 3:31-33
For the Lord will not cast off for ever: 32 But though he cause grief, yet will he have compassion according to the multitude of his mercies. 33 For he doth not afflict willingly nor grieve the children of men.
Psalms 18:2 The LORD is my rock, and my fortress, and my deliverer; my God, my strength, in whom I will trust; my buckler, and the horn of my salvation, and my high tower.

Micah 7:8-9
Rejoice not against me, O mine enemy: when I fall, I shall arise; when I sit in darkness, the LORD shall be a light unto me. 9 I will bear the indignation of the LORD, because I have sinned against him, until he plead my cause, and execute judgment for me: he will bring me forth to the light, and I shall behold his righteousness.

John 16:3 And these things will they do unto you, because they have not known the Father, nor me.

Holy Spirit

Proverbs 1:23 Turn you at my reproof: behold, I will pour out my spirit unto you, I will make known my words unto you.

John 14:16-17
And I will pray the Father, and he shall give you another Comforter, that he may abide with you for ever; 17 Even the Spirit of truth; whom the world cannot receive, because it seeth him not, neither knoweth him: but ye know him; for he dwelleth with you, and shall be in you.

John 7:38-39
He that believeth on me, as the scripture hath said, out of his belly shall flow rivers of living water. 39 (But this spake he of the Spirit, which they that believe on him should receive: for the Holy Ghost was not yet given; because that Jesus was not yet glorified.)

John 16:13 Howbeit when he, the Spirit of truth, is come, he will guide you into all truth: for he shall not speak of himself; but whatsoever he shall hear, that shall he speak: and he will show you things to come.

Isaiah 59:21
As for me, this is my covenant with them, saith the LORD; My spirit that is upon thee, and my words which I have put in thy mouth, shall not depart out of thy mouth, nor out of the mouth of

thy seed, nor out of the mouth of thy seed's seed, saith the LORD, from henceforth and for ever.

Luke 11:13 If ye then, being evil, know how to give good gifts unto your children: how much more shall your heavenly Father give the Holy Spirit to them that ask him?

John 4:14 But whosoever drinketh of the water that I shall give him shall never thirst; but the water that I shall give him shall be in him a well of water springing up into everlasting life.

Ezekiel 36:27 And I will put my spirit within you, and cause you to walk in my statutes, and ye shall keep my judgments, and do them.

Galatians 3:14 That the blessing of Abraham might come on the Gentiles through Jesus Christ; that we might receive the promise of the Spirit through faith.

1 John 2:27
But the anointing which ye have received of him abideth in you, and ye need not that any man teach you: but as the same anointing teacheth you of all things, and is truth, and is no lie, and even as it hath taught you, ye shall abide in him.

Romans 14:17 For the kingdom of God is not meat and drink; but righteousness, and peace, and joy in the Holy Ghost.

Romans 8:26-27
Likewise the Spirit also helpeth our infirmities: for we know not what we should pray for as we ought: but the Spirit itself maketh intercession for us with groanings which cannot be uttered. 27 And he that searcheth the hearts knoweth what is the mind of the Spirit, because he maketh intercession for the saints according to the will of God.

1 Corinthians 2:12 Now we have received, not the spirit of the world, but the spirit which is of God; that we might know the things that are freely given to us of God.

Romans 8:15 Therefore, brethren, we are debtors, not to the flesh, to live after the flesh.

Honesty

Leviticus 19:11 Ye shall not steal, neither deal falsely, neither lie one to another.

Micah 6:10-12
Are there yet the treasures of wickedness in the house of the wicked,
and the scant measure *that is* abominable? "Shall I count *them* pure
with the wicked balances, and with the bag of deceitful weights? [12] For
the rich men thereof are full of violence, and the inhabitants thereof
have spoken lies, and their tongue is deceitful in their mouth.

Leviticus 19:35 Ye shall do no unrighteousness in judgment, in meteyard, in weight, or in measure.

Proverbs 11:1 A false balance *is* abomination to the LORD: but a just weight is his delight.

Deuteronomy 25:15-16
But thou shalt have a perfect and just weight, a perfect and just
measure shalt thou have: that thy days may he lengthened in the
land which the LORD thy God giveth thee. [16] For all that do such
things, *and* all that do unrighteously, *are* an abomination unto the
LORD thy God.

1 Thessalonians 4:6-7
That no *man* go beyond and defraud his brother in *any* matter:
because that the Lord is the avenger of all such, as we also have

forewarned you and testified. For God hath not called us unto uncleanness, but unto holiness.

Colossians 3:9-10 Lie not one to another, seeing that ye have put off the old man with his deeds; [10] And have put on the new *man,* which is renewed in knowledge after the image of him that created him.

Proverbs 3:27 Withhold not good from them to whom it is due, when it is in the power of thine hand to do *it.*

Leviticus 25:14 And if thou sell ought unto thy neighbour, or buyest *ought* of thy; neighbour's hand, ye shall not oppress one another:

Isaiah 33:15-16

He that walketh righteously, and speaketh uprightly; he that despiseth the gain of oppressions, that shaketh his hands from holding of bribes that stoppeth his ears from hearing of blood, and shutteth his eyes from seeing evil; [16] He shall dwell on high: his place of defence *shall be* thy munitions of rocks: bread shall be given him; his waters *shall he* sure.

Proverbs 16:8 Better is a little with righteousness than great revenues without right.

Hope

Psalms 42:11 Why art thou cast down, O my soul? And why art thou disquieted within me? Hope thou in God: for I shall yet praise him, who is the health of my countenance, and my God.

1Peter 1:21 Who by him do believe in God that raised him up from the dead, and gave him glory; that your faith and hope might be in God.

1Peter 1:13 Wherefore gird up the loins of your mind, be sober, and hope to the end for the grace that is to be brought unto you at the revelation of Jesus Christ.

1 John 3:3 And every man that hath this hope in him purifieth himself, even as he is pure.

Proverbs 14:32 The wicked is driven away in his wickedness: but the righteous hath hope in his death.

Colossians 1:5 For the hope which is laid up for you in heaven, whereof ye heard before in the word of the truth of the gospel.

Colossians 1:27 "…which is Christ in you, the hope of glory."

Psalms 31:24 Be of good courage, and he shall strengthen your heart, all ye that hope in the LORD.

Psalms 71:5 For thou art my hope, O Lord GOD: thou art my trust from my youth.

1 Peter 1:3 Blessed be the God and Father of our Lord Jesus Christ, which according to his abundant mercy hath begotten us again unto a lively hope by the resurrection of Jesus Christ from the dead.

Hospitality

1Peter 4:9-10 Use hospitality one to another without grudging. 10 As every man hath received the gift, even so minister the same one to another, as good stewards of the manifold grace of God.

James 2:15-16
If a brother or sister be naked, and destitute of daily food, 16 And one of you say unto them, Depart in peace, be ye warmed and filled; notwithstanding ye give them not those things which are needful to the body; what doth it profit?

Mark 9:41 For whosoever shall give you a cup of water to drink in my name, because ye belong to Christ, verily I say unto you, he shall not lose his reward

Acts 20:35 I have showed you all things, how that so labouring ye ought to support the weak, and to remember the words of the Lord Jesus, how he said, It is more blessed to give than to receive.

1 John 3:17 But whoso hath this world's good, and seeth his brother have need, and shutteth up his bowels of compassion from him, how dwelleth the love of God in him?

Romans 12:13 Distributing to the necessity of saints; given to hospitality.

2 Corinthians 8:13-14

For I mean not that other men be eased, and ye burdened: 14 But by equality, that now at this time your abundance may be a supply for their want, that their abundance also may be a supply for your want: that there may be equality.

Matthew 25:35-36
For I was an hungered, and ye gave me meat: I was thirsty, and ye gave me drink: I was a stranger, and ye took me in: 36 Naked, and ye clothed me: I was sick, and ye visited me: I was in prison, and ye came unto me.

Matthew 25:40 And the King shall answer and say unto them, Verily I say unto you, Inasmuch as ye have done it unto one of the least of these my brethren, ye have done it unto me.

Hebrews 13:2 Be not forgetful to entertain strangers: for thereby some have entertained angels unawares.

Humility

Matthew 18:4 Whosoever therefore shall humble himself as this little child, the same is greatest in the kingdom of heaven.

Psalms 10:17 LORD, thou hast heard the desire of the humble: thou wilt prepare their heart, thou wilt cause thine ear to hear:

Matthew 23:12 And whosoever shall exalt himself shall be abased; and he that shall humble himself shall be exalted.

Job 22:29 When men are cast down, then thou shalt say, There is lifting up; and he shall save the humble person.

Proverbs 16:19 Better it is to be of an humble spirit with the lowly, than to divide the spoil with the proud.

Proverbs 3:34 Surely he scorneth the scorners: but he giveth grace unto the lowly.

James 4:6 But he giveth more grace. Wherefore he saith, God resisteth the proud, but giveth grace unto the humble.

Psalms 9:12 When he maketh inquisition for blood, he remembereth them: he forgetteth not the cry of the humble.

Proverbs 22:4 By humility and the fear of the LORD are riches, and honour, and life.

Proverbs 15:33 The fear of the LORD is the instruction of wisdom; and before honour is humility.

Proverbs 29:23 A man's pride shall bring him low: but honour shall uphold the humble in spirit.

1 Peter 5:6 Humble yourselves therefore under the mighty hand of God, that he may exalt you in due time.

Jealously

Deuteronomy 5:21
Neither shalt thou desire thy neighbour's wife, neither shalt thou covet thy neighbour's house, his field, or his manservant, or his maidservant,his ox, or his ass, or any *thing* that is thy neighbour's.

James 3:16 For where envying and strife is, there *is* confusion and every evil work.

James 4:5 Do ye think that the scripture saith in vain, the spirit that dwelleth in us lusteth to envy?

Psalms 37:7 Rest in the LORD, and wait patiently for him: fret not thyself because of him who prospereth in his way, because of the man who bringeth wicked devices to pass.

Psalms 10:3 For the wicked boasteth of his heart's desire, and blesseth the covetous, *whom* the LORD abhorreth.

Proverbs 3:31 Envy thou not the oppressor, and choose none of his ways.

Proverbs 14:30 A sound heart is the life of the flesh: but envy the rottenness of the bones.

Proverbs 27:4 Wrath *is* cruel, and anger is outrageous; but who is able to stand before envy?

Ecclesiastes 4:4 Again, I considered all travail, and every right work, that for this a man is envied of his neighbour. This is also vanity and vexation of spirit.

Joy

Isaiah 55:12 For ye shall go out with joy, and be led forth with peace: the mountains and the hills shall break forth before you into singing, and all the trees of the field shall clap their hands.

Psalm 89:15-16
Blessed is the people that know the joyful sound: they shall walk, O LORD, in the light of thy countenance. 16 In thy name shall they rejoice all the day: and in thy righteousness shall they be exalted.

Psalm 118:15 The voice of rejoicing and salvation is in the tabernacles of the righteous: the right hand of the LORD doeth valiantly.

Psalms 4:7 Thou hast put gladness in my heart, more than in the time that their corn and their wine increased.

Psalms 126:5-6 They that sow in tears shall reap in joy. 6 He that goeth forth and weepeth, bearing precious seed, shall doubtless come again with rejoicing, bringing his sheaves with him.

Psalms 97:11-12 Light is sown for the righteous, and gladness for the upright in heart. 12 Rejoice in the LORD, ye righteous; and give thanks at the remembrance of his holiness.

Job 22:26 For then shalt thou have thy delight in the Almighty, and shalt lift up thy face unto God.

John 15:11 These things have I spoken unto you, that my joy might remain in you, and that your joy might be full.

Habakkuk 3:18 Yet I will rejoice in the LORD, I will joy in the God of my salvation.

Isaiah 51:11 Therefore the redeemed of the LORD shall return, and come with singing unto Zion; and everlasting joy shall be upon their head: they shall obtain gladness and joy; and sorrow and mourning shall flee away.

Psalms33:21 For our heart shall rejoice in him, because we have trusted in his holy name.

1Peter 1:8 Whom having not seen, ye love; in whom, though now ye see him not, yet believing, ye rejoice with joy unspeakable and full of glory.

Nehemiah 8:10
Then he said unto them, Go your way, eat the fat, and drink the sweet, and send portions unto them for whom nothing is prepared: for this day is holy unto our Lord: neither be ye sorry; for the joy of the LORD is your strength.

Isaiah 61:10
I will greatly rejoice in the LORD, my soul shall be joyful in my God; for he hath clothed me with the garments of salvation, he hath covered me with the robe of righteousness, as a bridegroom decketh himself with ornaments, and as a bride adorneth herself with her jewels.

Isaiah 41:16 Thou shalt fan them, and the wind shall carry them away, and the whirlwind shall scatter them: and thou shalt rejoice in the LORD, and shalt glory in the Holy One of Israel.

Psalms 64:10 The righteous shall be glad in the LORD, and shall trust in him; and all the upright in heart shall glory.

Psalms 63:5 My soul shall be satisfied as with marrow and fatness; and my mouth shall praise thee with joyful lips.

Psalms 68:3 But let the righteous be glad; let them rejoice before God: yea, let them exceedingly rejoice.

John 16:22b "...But I will see you again, and your heart shall rejoice, and your joy no man taketh from you."

Laziness

1 Thessalonians 4:11-12
And that ye study to be quiet, and to do your own business, and to work with your own hands, as we commanded you; 12 That ye may walk honestly toward them that are without, and that ye may have lack of nothing.

Romans 12:11 Not slothful in business; fervent in spirit; serving the Lord.

Proverbs 28:19 He that tilleth his land shall have plenty of bread: but he that followeth after vain persons shall have poverty enough.

Proverbs 13:4 The soul of the sluggard desireth, and hath nothing: but the soul of the diligent shall be made fat.

Proverbs 10:4-5 He becometh poor that dealeth with a slack hand: but the hand of the diligent maketh rich. 5 He that gathereth in summer is a wise son: but he that sleepeth in harvest is a son that causeth shame.

2 Thessalonians 3:10-12
For even when we were with you, this we commanded you, that if any would not work, neither should he eat. 11 For we hear that there are some which walk among you disorderly, working not at all, but are busybodies. 12 Now them that are such we command and

exhort by our Lord Jesus Christ, that with quietness they work, and eat their own bread.

Proverbs 13:23 Much food is in the tillage of the poor: but there is that is destroyed for want of judgment.

2 Timothy 2:6 The husbandman that laboureth must be first partaker of the fruits.

Ephesians 4:28 Let him that stole steal no more: but rather let him labour, working with his hands the thing which is good, that he may have to give to him that needeth.

Proverbs 24:30-34

I went by the field of the slothful, and by the vineyard of the man void of understanding; 31 And, lo, it was all grown over with thorns, and nettles had covered the face thereof, and the stone wall thereof was broken down. 32 Then I saw, and considered it well: I looked upon it, and received instruction. 33 Yet a little sleep, a little slumber, a little folding of the hands to sleep: 34 So shall thy poverty come as one that travelleth; and thy want as an armed man.

Proverbs 20:13 Love not sleep, lest thou come to poverty; open thine eyes, and thou shalt be satisfied with bread.

Proverbs 15:19 The way of the slothful man is as an hedge of thorns: but the way of the righteous is made plain.

Proverbs 21:5 The thoughts of the diligent tend only to plenteousness; but of every one that is hasty only to want.

Proverbs 12:24 The hand of the diligent shall bear rule: but the slothful shall be under tribute.

Proverbs 12:11 He that tilleth his land shall be satisfied with bread: but he that followeth vain persons is void of understanding.

Proverbs 27:23 Be thou diligent to know the state of thy flocks, and look well to thy herds.

Proverbs 27:27 And thou shalt have goats' milk enough for thy food, for the food of thy household, and for the maintenance for thy maidens.

Ecclesiastes 5:18-19
Behold that which I have seen: it is good and comely for one to eat and to drink, and to enjoy the good of all his labour that he taketh under the sun all the days of his life, which God giveth him: for it is his portion. 19 Every man also to whom God hath given riches and wealth, and hath given him power to eat thereof, and to take his portion, and to rejoice in his labour; this is the gift of God.

Loneliness

John 14:18 I will not leave you comfortless: I will come to you.

Isaiah 58:9 Then shalt thou call, and the LORD shall answer; thou shalt cry, and he shall say, Here I am. If thou take away from the midst of thee the yoke, the putting forth of the finger, and speaking vanity.

Isaiah 43:4 Then shalt thou call, and the LORD shall answer; thou shalt cry, and he shall say, Here I am. If thou take away from the midst of thee the yoke, the putting forth of the finger, and speaking vanity.

2 Corinthians 6:13 And will be a Father unto you, and ye shall be my sons and daughters, saith the Lord Almighty.

Genesis 28:15 And, behold, I am with thee, and will keep thee in all places whither thou goest, and will bring thee again into this land; for I will not leave thee, until I have done that which I have spoken to thee of.

Colossians 2:10 And ye are complete in him, which is the head of all principality and power:

Psalms 40:17 But I am poor and needy; yet the Lord thinketh upon me: thou art my help and my deliverer; make no tarrying, O my God.

Long life

Isaiah 46:4 And even to your old age I am he; and even to hoar hairs will I carry you: I have made, and I will bear; even I will carry, and will deliver you.

Job 12:12-13 With the ancient is wisdom; and in length of days understanding. 13 With him is wisdom and strength, he hath counsel and understanding.

Proverbs 20:29 The glory of young men is their strength: and the beauty of old men is the grey head.

Proverbs 17:6 Children's children are the crown of old men; and the glory of children are their fathers.

Job 5:26 Thou shalt come to thy grave in a full age, like as a shock of corn cometh in in his season.

Job 11:17 And thine age shall be clearer than the noonday; thou shalt shine forth, thou shalt be as the morning.

Psalms 71:9 Cast me not off in the time of old age; forsake me not when my strength faileth.

Titus2:1-5 But speak thou the things which become sound doctrine: 2 That the aged men be sober, grave, temperate, sound in faith, in charity, in patience. 3 The aged women likewise, that they be in behaviour as becometh holiness, not false accusers, not given to much wine, teachers of good things; 4 That they may teach the young women to be sober, to love their husbands, to love their children, 5 To be discreet, chaste, keepers at home, good, obedient to their own husbands, that the word of God be not blasphemed.

Psalms 71:17-18
O God, thou hast taught me from my youth: and hitherto have I declared thy wondrous works. 18 Now also when I am old and greyheaded, O God, forsake me not; until I have showed thy strength unto this generation, and thy power to every one that is to come.

Psalms 39:4-5
LORD, make me to know mine end, and the measure of my days, what it is; that I may know how frail I am. 5 Behold, thou hast made my days as an handbreadth; and mine age is as nothing before thee: verily every man at his best state is altogether vanity. Selah.

Deuteronomy 5:33 Ye shall walk in all the ways which the LORD your God hath commanded you, that ye may live, and that it may be well with you, and that ye may prolong your days in the land which ye shall possess.

Proverbs 3:1-2 My son, forget not my law; but let thine heart keep my commandments: 2 For length of days, and long life, and peace, shall they add to thee.

Deuteronomy 6:2
That thou mightest fear the LORD thy God, to keep all his statutes and his commandments, which I command thee, thou, and thy son, and thy son's son, all the days of thy life; and that thy days may be prolonged.

Psalms 91:16 With long life will I satisfy him, and show him my salvation.

Proverbs 10:27 The fear of the LORD prolongeth days: but the years of the wicked shall be shortened.

Proverbs 9:11 For by me thy days shall be multiplied, and the years of thy life shall be increased.

Love, brotherly

John 13:34-35 A new commandment I give unto you, that ye love one another; as I have loved you, that ye also love one another. 35 By this shall all men know that ye are my disciples, if ye have love one to another.

Romans 12:9-10 Let love be without dissimulation. Abhor that which is evil; cleave to that which is good. 10 Be kindly affectioned one to another with brotherly love; in honour preferring one another.

1 Thessalonians 4:9 But as touching brotherly love ye need not that I write unto you: for ye yourselves are taught of God to love one another.

1 John 2:10 He that loveth his brother abideth in the light, and there is none occasion of stumbling in him.

1 Peter 1:22 Seeing ye have purified your souls in obeying the truth through the Spirit unto unfeigned love of the brethren, see that ye love one another with a pure heart fervently.

1 John 4:7-8 Beloved, let us love one another: for love is of God; and every one that loveth is born of God, and knoweth God. 8 He that loveth not knoweth not God; for God is love.

1 John 3:18 My little children, let us not love in word, neither in tongue; but in deed and in truth.

1 John 4:11 Beloved, if God so loved us, we ought also to love one another.

Colossians 3:12-13

Put on therefore, as the elect of God, holy and beloved, bowels of mercies, kindness, humbleness of mind, meekness, longsuffering; 13 Forbearing one another, and forgiving one another, if any man have a quarrel against any: even as Christ forgave you, so also do ye.

Love, God's

John 3:16 For God so loved the world, that he gave his only begotten Son, that whosoever believeth in him should not perish, but have everlasting life.

Deuteronomy 7:13
And he will love thee, and bless thee, and multiply thee: he will also bless the fruit of thy womb, and the fruit of thy land, thy corn, and thy wine, and thine oil, the increase of thy kale, and the flocks of thy sheep in the land which he sware unto thy fathers to give thee.

Psalms 146:8 The LORD openeth *the eyes of* the blind: the LORD raiseth them that are bowed down: the LORD loveth the righteous:

Proverbs 15:9 The way of the wicked *is* an abomination unto the LORD: but he loveth him that followeth after righteousness.

Isaiah 62:5 For *as* a young man marrieth a virgin, so shall thy sons marry thee: and *as* the bridegroom rejoiceth over the bride, so shall thy God rejoice over thee.

Jeremiah 31:3 The LORD hath appeared of old unto me, *saying,* Yea, I have loved thee with an everlasting love: therefore with lovingkindness have drawn thee.

Zephaniah 3:17 The LORD thy God in the midst of thee is mighty; he will save, he will rejoice over thee with joy; he will rest in his love, he will joy over the with singing.

Hosea 14:4 I will heal their backsliding, I will love them freely: for mine anger is turned away from him.

Jeremiah 32:41 Yea, I will rejoice over them to do them good, and I will plant them in this land assuredly with my whole heart and with my whole soul.

Ephesians 2:4-7
But God, who is rich in mercy, for his great love wherewith he loved us, [5] Even when we were dead in sins, hath quickened us together with Christ, (by grace ye are saved;) [6] And hath raised *us* up together, and made *us* sit together in heavenly *places* in Christ Jesus: That in the ages to come he might show the exceeding riches of his grace in *his* kindness toward us through Christ Jesus.

1 John 4:10 Herein is love, not that we loved God, but that he loved us, and sent his Son *to be* the propitiation for our sins.

John 16:27 For the Father himself loveth you, because ye have loved me, and have believed that I came out from God.

1 John 4:16 And we have known and believed the love that God hath to us. God is love; and he that dwelleth in love dwelleth in God. and God in him.

1John 4:19 We love him, because he first loved us.

John 17:26 And I have declared unto them thy name, and will declare *it:* that the love wherewith thou hast loved me may be in them, and I in them.

John 17:23 I in them, and thou in me, that they may be made perfect in one; and that the world may know that thou bast sent me, and hast loved them, as thou hast loved me.

2 Thessalonians 2:16-17
Now our Lord Jesus Christ himself, and God, even our Father, whitch hath loved us, and hath given *us* everlasting consolation and good hope through grace, 17 Comfort your hearts, and stablish you in every good word and work.

Deuteronomy 11:13-15
LORD your God, and to serve him with all your heart and with all your soul, 14 That I will give you the rain of your land in his due season, the first rain and the latter rain, that thou mayest gather in thy corn, and thy wine, and thine oil. 15 And I will send grass in thy fields for thy cattle, that thou mayest eat and be full.

Lust

James 4:1-3
From whence *come* wars and fightings among you? *Come they* not hence, *even* of your lusts that war in your members? [2] Ye lust, and have not: ye kill, and desire to have, and cannot obtain: ye fight and war, yet ye have not, because ye ask not. Ye ask, and receive not, because ye ask amiss, that ye may consume *it* upon your lusts.

James 4:4 Ye adulterers and adulteresses, know ye not that the friendship of the world is enmity with God? whosoever therefore will be a friend of the world is the enemy of God.

John 2:16-17 For all that is in the world, the lust of the flesh, and the lust of the eyes, and the pride of life, is not of the Father, but is of the world. [17] And the world passeth away, and the lust thereof: but he that doeth the will of God abideth for ever.

Matthew 5:27-28 Ye have heard that it was said by them of old time, Thou shalt not commit adultery: [28] But I say unto you, that whosoever looketh on a woman to lust after her hath committed adultery with her already in his heart.

Proverbs 6:25-29
Lust not after her beauty in thine heart; neither let her take thee with her eyelids. [26] For by means of a whorish woman *a man is brought* to a piece of bread: and the adulteress will hunt for the precious life. [27] Can a man take fire in his bosom, and his clothes not be burned?

[28] Can one go upon hot coals, and his feet not be burned? [29] So he that goeth in to his neighbour's wife; whosoever toucheth her shall not be innocent.

James 4:7-8 Submit yourselves therefore to God. Resist the devil, and he will flee from you. [8] Draw nigh to God, and he will draw nigh to you. Cleanse *your* hands, *ye* sinners; and purify *your* hearts, *ye* double minded.

1 Peter 2:11 Dearly beloved, I beseech *you* as strangers and pilgrims, abstain from fleshly lusts, which war against the soul.

Peter 1:14-16 As obedient children, not fashioning yourselves according to the former lusts in your ignorance: [15] But as he which hath called you is holy, so be ye holy in all manner of conversation; [16]Because it is written, Be y holy; for I am holy.

2 Timothy 2:22 Flee also youthful lusts: but follow righteousness, faith, charity, peace with them that call on the Lord out of a pure heart.

Titus 3:3-5
For we ourselves also were sometimes foolish, disobedient, deceived serving divers lusts and pleasures, living in malice and envy, hateful *and* hating one another. But after that the kindness and love of Goy our Saviour toward man appeared, [5] Not by works of righteousness which we have done, but according to his mercy he saved us, by the washing of regeneration, and renewing of the Holy Ghost.

Ephesians 2:3-6 Among whom also we all had our conversation in times past in the lust of our flesh, fulfilling the desires of the flesh and of the mind; and were by nature the children of wrath, even as others. [4] But God, who is rich in mercy, for his great love wherewith he loved us, [5] Even when we were dead in sins, hath quickened us together with Christ, (by grace ye are saved;) [6] And hath raised *us* up together, and made *us* sit together in heavenly *places* in Christ Jesus.

Titus 2:11-12 For the grace of God that bringeth salvation bath appeared to all men, 12 Teaching us that, denying ungodliness and worldly lusts, we should live soberly, righteously, and godly, in this present world.

James 1:13 Let no man say when he is tempted, I am tempted of God: for God cannot be tempted with evil, neither tempteth he any man.

Galatians 5:24 And they that are Christ's have crucified the flesh with the affections and lusts.

Jude 1:18-20
How that they told you there should be mockers in the last time, who should walk after their own ungodly lusts. These be they who separate themselves, sensual, having not the Spirit. [20] But ye, beloved, building up yourselves on your most holy faith, praying in the Holy Ghost.

Galatians 5:16-17
This I say then, Walk in the Spirit, and ye shall not fulfil the lust of the flesh. '[7] For the flesh lusteth against the Spirit, and the Spirit against the flesh: and these are contrary the one to the other: so that ye cannot do the things that ye would.

Romans 6:11-12
Likewise reckon ye also yourselves to be dead indeed unto sin, but alive unto God through Jesus Christ our Lord. '[2] Let not sin therefore reign in your mortal body, that ye should obey it in the lusts thereof.

2 Peter 1:4 Whereby are given unto us exceeding great and precious promises: that by these ye might be partakers of the divine nature, having escaped the corruption that is in the world through lust.

Lying

Colossians 3:9-10 Lie not one to another, seeing that ye have put off the old man with his deeds; 10 And have put on the new man, which is renewed in knowledge after the image of him that created him.

Leviticus 19:12 And ye shall not swear by my name falsely, neither shalt thou profane the name of thy God: I am the LORD.

Proverbs 25:18 A man that beareth false witness against his neighbour is a maul, and a sword, and a sharp arrow.

Zechariah 8:17 And let none of you imagine evil in your hearts against his neighbour; and love no false oath: for all these are things that I hate, saith the LORD.

Proverbs 14:5 A faithful witness will not lie: but a false witness will utter lies.

1 Kings 22:16 And the king said unto him, How many times shall I adjure thee that thou tell me nothing but that which is true in the name of the LORD?

Proverbs 19:5 A false witness shall not be unpunished, and he that speaketh lies shall not escape.

Deuteronomy 19:16-19
If a false witness rise up against any man to testify against him that which is wrong; 17 Then both the men, between whom the controversy is, shall stand before the LORD, before the priests and the judges, which shall be in those days; 18 And the judges shall make diligent inquisition: and, behold, if the witness be a false witness, and hath testified falsely against his brother; 19 Then shall ye do unto him, as he had thought to have done unto his brother: so shalt thou put the evil away from among you.

Revelation 21:8
But the fearful, and unbelieving, and the abominable, and murderers, and whoremongers, and sorcerers, and idolaters, and all liars, shall have their part in the lake which burneth with fire and brimstone: which is the second death.

Proverbs 19:9 A false witness shall not be unpunished, and he that speaketh lies shall perish.

Proverbs 24:28 Be not a witness against thy neighbour without cause; and deceive not with thy lips.

Psalms 58:3 The wicked are estranged from the womb: they go astray as soon as they be born, speaking lies.

James 3:14 But if ye have bitter envying and strife in your hearts, glory not, and lie not against the truth.

Exodus 23:1 Thou shalt not raise a false report: put not thine hand with the wicked to be an unrighteous witness.

Proverbs 12:19 The lip of truth shall be established for ever: but a lying tongue is but for a moment.

Meekness

Matthew 5:5 Blessed are the meek: for they shall inherit the earth.

Isaiah 11:4
But with righteousness shall he judge the poor, and reprove with equity for the meek of the earth: and he shall smite the earth with the rod of his mouth, and with the breath of his lips shall he slay the wicked.

Psalms 22:26 The meek shall eat and be satisfied: they shall praise the LORD that seek him: your heart shall live for ever.

Psalms 149:4 For the LORD taketh pleasure in his people: he will beautify the meek with salvation.

Isaiah 29:19 The meek also shall increase their joy in the LORD, and the poor among men shall rejoice in the Holy One of Israel.

Psalms 147:6 The LORD lifteth up the meek: he casteth the wicked down to the ground.

Psalms 25:9 The meek will he guide in judgment: and the meek will he teach his way.

1Peter 3:4 But let it be the hidden man of the heart, in that which is not corruptible, even the ornament of a meek and quiet spirit, which is in the sight of God of great price.

Zephaniah 2:3 And, behold, the angel that talked with me went forth, and another angel went out to meet him.

Psalms 37:11 But the meek shall inherit the earth; and shall delight themselves in the abundance of peace.

Proverbs 15:1 A soft answer turneth away wrath: but grievous words stir up anger.

Mercy

Isaiah 30:18
And therefore will the LORD wait, that he may be gracious unto you, and therefore will he be exalted, that he may have mercy upon you: for the LORD is a God of judgment: blessed are all they that wait for him.

Job 11:6 And that he would show thee the secrets of wisdom, that they are double to that which is! Know therefore that God exacteth of thee less than thine iniquity deserveth.

Psalms 103:13 Like as a father pitieth his children, so the LORD pitieth them that fear him.

Psalms 103:17 But the mercy of the LORD is from everlasting to everlasting upon them that fear him, and his righteousness unto children's children.

Exodus 33:19 And he said, I will make all my goodness pass before thee, and I will proclaim the name of the LORD before thee; and will be gracious to whom I will be gracious, and will show mercy on whom I will show mercy.

Hosea 2:23 And I will sow her unto me in the earth; and I will have mercy upon her that had not obtained mercy; and I will say to them which were not my people, Thou art my people; and they shall say, Thou art my God.

Isaiah 60:10 And the sons of strangers shall build up thy walls, and their kings shall minister unto thee: for in my wrath I smote thee, but in my favour have I had mercy on thee.

Isaiah 48:9 For my name's sake will I defer mine anger, and for my praise will I refrain for thee, that I cut thee not off.

Money

Proverbs 23:4 Labour not to be rich: cease from thine own wisdom.

Proverbs 23:5 Wilt thou set thine eyes upon that which is not? for *riches* certainly make themselves wings; they fly away as an eagle toward heaven.

Psalms 37:16 A little that a righteous man hath is better than the riches of many wicked.

James 2:5 Hearken, my beloved brethren, Hath not God chosen the poor of this world rich in faith, and heirs of the kingdom which he hath promised to them that love him?

Ecclesiast 14:6 Better is an handful *with* quietness, than both the hands full *with* travail and vexation of spirit.

Psalms 12:5 For the oppression of the poor, for the sighing of the needy, now will I arise, saith the LORD; I will set *him* in safety *from him that* puffeth at him.

Proverbs 17:5 Whoso mocketh the poor reproacheth his Maker: *and* he that is glad at calamities shall not be unpunished.

Proverbs 22:22 Rob not the poor, because he is poor: neither oppress the afflicted in the gate:

1 Timothy 6:17-19
Charge them that are rich in this world, that they be not highminded, nor trust in uncertain riches, but in the living God, who giveth us richly all things to enjoy; [18] That they do good, that they be rich in good works, ready to distribute, willing to communicate; [19] Laying up it store for themselves a good foundation against the time to come, that they may lay hold on eternal life.

Ecclesiastes 5:12-14
The sleep of a laboring man is sweet, whether he eat little or much; but the abundance of the rich will not suffer him to sleep. [13] There is sore evil *which I* have seen under the sun, *namely,* riches kept for the owners thereof to their hurt. [14] But those riches perish by evil travail; and he begetteth a son, and *there is* nothing in his hand.

Deuteronomy 8:18 But thou shalt remember the LORD thy God: for *it is* he that giveth thee power to get wealth, that he may establish his covenant which he sware unto thy fathers, as *it is* this day.

Psalms 9:18 For the needy shall not alway be forgotten: the expectation of the pool shall *not* perish for ever.

Job 5:15-16 But he saveth the poor from the sword, from their mouth, and from the hand of the mighty. [16] So the poor hath hope, and iniquity stoppeth he] mouth.

Proverbs 11:28 He that trusteth in his riches shall fall: but the righteous shall flourish a: a branch.

Proverbs 28:20 A faithful man shall abound with blessings: but he that maketh haste to be rich shall not be innocent.

Proverbs 11:4 Riches profit not in the day of wrath: but righteousness delivereth from death.

Ezekiel 7:19
They shall cast their silver in the streets, and their gold shall be to the chief Musician, A Psalm of David. Blessed *is* he that consideret removed: their silver and their gold shall not be able to deliver them in the day of the wrath of the LORD: they shall not satisfy their souls, neither fill their bowels: because it is the stumblingblock of their iniquity.

Proverbs 13:7 There is that maketh himself rich, yet *hath* nothing: *there is* that maketh himself poor, yet *hath* great riches.

Ecclesiast 5:10 He that loveth silver shall not be satisfied with silver; nor he that loveth abundance with increase: this *is* also vanity.

Proverbs 22:16 He that oppresseth the poor to increase his *riches, and* he that giveth to the rich, *shall* surely *came* to want.

Proverbs 28:22 He that hasteth to be rich *hath* an evil eye, and considereth not that poverty shall come upon him.

Proverbs 22:2 The rich and poor meet together: the LORD *is* the maker of them all.

Job 36:15 He delivereth the poor in his affliction, and openeth their ears in oppression.

Proverbs 15:16 Better is little with the fear of the LORD than great treasure and trouble therewith.

Proverbs 28:6 Better *is* the poor that walketh in his uprightness, than *he that is* perverse *in his* ways, though he *be* rich.

Psalms 41:1 To the chief Musician, A Psalm of David. Blessed is he that considereth the poor: the LORD will deliver him in time of trouble.

Matthew 5:19
Whosoever therefore shall break one of these least commandments, and shall teach men so, he shall be called the least in the kingdom of heaven: but whosoever shall do and teach them, the same shall be called great in the kingdom of heaven.

Matthew 7:24-25
Therefore whosoever heareth these sayings of mine, and doeth them, will liken him unto a wise man, which built his house upon a rock:
[2] And the rain descended, and the floods came, and the winds blew, and beat upon that house; and it fell not: for it was founded upon a rock.

Job 36:11 If they obey and serve *him,* they shall spend their days in prosperity and their years in pleasures.

Romans 8:28 And we know that all things work together for good to them that love God, to them who are the called according to *his* purpose.

John 15:10 If ye keep my commandments, ye shall abide in my love; even as I have kept my Father's commandments, and abide in his love.

John 13:17 If ye know these things, happy are ye if ye do them.

James 1:25 But whoso looketh into the perfect law of liberty, and continuet *therein,* he being not a forgetful hearer, but a doer of the work, this man shall be blessed in his deed.

1 John 3:22 And whatsoever we ask, we receive of him, because we keep hi commandments, and do those things that are pleasing in his sight.

Romans 2:13 For not the hearers of the law *are* just before God, but the doers of the law shall be justified.

Matthew 12:50 For whosoever shall do the will of my Father which is in heaven, the same is my brother, and sister, and mother.
1 John 2:17 And the world passeth away, and the lust thereof: but he that doeth the will of God abideth for ever.

Matthew 7:21 Not every one that saith unto me, Lord, Lord, shall enter into the kingdom of heaven; but he that doeth the will of my Father which is in heaven.

Psalms 106:3 Blessed *are* they that keep judgment, *and* he that doeth righteousness at all times.

Hebrews 5:9 And being made perfect, he became the author of eternal salvation unto all them that obey him.

John 8:51 Verily, verily, I say unto you, if a man keep my saying, he shall never see death.

Patience

James 5:7-8
Be patient therefore, brethren, unto the coming of the Lord. Behold, the husbandman waiteth for the precious fruit of the earth, and hath long patience for it, until he receive the early and latter rain. 8
Be ye also patient; stablish your hearts: for the coming of the Lord draweth nigh.

1 Peter 2:20 For what glory is it, if, when ye be buffeted for your faults, ye shall take it patiently? But if, when ye do well, and suffer for it, ye take it patiently, this is acceptable with God.

Galatians 6:9 And let us not be weary in well doing: for in due season we shall reap, if we faint not.

Hebrews 10:23 Let us hold fast the profession of our faith without wavering; (for he is faithful that promised;)

Matthew 24:13 But he that shall endure unto the end, the same shall be saved.

Hebrews 6:12 That ye be not slothful, but followers of them who through faith and patience inherit the promises.

Hebrews 10:36 For ye have need of patience, that, after ye have done the will of God, ye might receive the promise.

James 1:2-4
My brethren, count it all joy when ye fall into divers temptations;
3 Knowing this, that the trying of your faith worketh patience. 4
But let patience have her perfect work, that ye may be perfect and entire, wanting nothing.

Romans 5:3-4 And not only so, but we glory in tribulations also: knowing that tribulation worketh patience; 4 And patience, experience; and experience, hope:

Peace

Isaiah 53:5 But he was wounded for our transgressions; he was bruised for our iniquities: the chastisement of our peace was upon him; and with his stripes we are healed.

Isaiah 57:19 "… Peace, peace to him that is far off, and to him that is near, saith the LORD; and I will heal him."

Colossians 3:15 And let the peace of God rule in your hearts, to the which also ye are called in one body; and be ye thankful.

Psalms 85:8
I will both lay me down in peace, and sleep: for thou, LORD, only makest me dwell in safety.
Will hear what God the LORD will speak: for he will speak peace unto his people, and to his saints: but let them not turn again to folly.

Philippians 4:7 And the peace of God, which passeth all understanding, shall keep your hearts and minds through Christ Jesus.

Isaiah 32:17 And the work of righteousness shall be peace; and the effect of righteousness quietness and assurance for ever.

Luke 7:50 And he said to the woman, Thy faith hath saved thee; go in peace.

Psalm 37:37 Mark the perfect man, and behold the upright: for the end of that man is peace.

2 Thessalonians 3:16 Now the Lord of peace himself give you peace always by all means. The Lord be with you all.

John 14:27 Peace I leave with you, my peace I give unto you: not as the world giveth, give I unto you. Let not your heart be troubled, neither let it be afraid.

Romans 5:1 Therefore being justified by faith, we have peace with God through our Lord Jesus Christ:

Luke 7:48-50; See Luke 7:36-50 And he said unto her, Thy sins are forgiven. 49 And they that sat at meat with him began to say within themselves, Who is this that forgiveth sins also? 50 And he said to the woman, Thy faith hath saved thee; go in peace.

Psalms 4:8 I will both lay me down in peace, and sleep: for thou, LORD, only makest me dwell in safety.

Romans 8:6 For to be carnally minded is death; but to be spiritually minded is life and peace.

Galatians 5:22:23 But the fruit of the Spirit is love, joy, peace, longsuffering, gentleness, goodness, faith, 23 Meekness, temperance: against such there is no law.

Isaiah 26:3-4 Thou wilt keep him in perfect peace, whose mind is stayed on thee: because he trusteth in thee. 4 Trust ye in the LORD for ever: for in the LORD JEHOVAH is everlasting strength:

Philippians 4:6-7 Be careful for nothing; but in every thing by prayer and supplication with thanksgiving let your requests be made known unto God. 7 And the peace of God, which passeth all understanding, shall keep your hearts and minds through Christ Jesus.

Isaiah 57:2
For unto us a child is born, unto us a son is given: and the government shall be upon his shoulder: and his name shall be called Wonderful, Counsellor, The mighty God, The everlasting Father, The Prince of Peace. He shall enter into peace: they shall rest in their beds, each one walking in his uprightness.

Isaiah 57:19-20; See Isaiah 14-21 I create the fruit of the lips; Peace, peace to him that is far off, and to him that is near, saith the LORD; and I will heal him. 20 But the wicked are like the troubled sea, when it cannot rest, whose waters cast up mire and dirt.

Isaiah 57:21 There is no peace, saith my God, to the wicked.

Jeremiah 8:11-12 For they have healed the hurt of the daughter of my people slightly, saying, Peace, peace; when there is no peace.12 Were they ashamed when they had committed abomination? Nay, they were not at all ashamed, neither could they blush: therefore shall they fall among them that fall: in the time of their visitation they shall be cast down, saith the LORD.

Poverty

Psalms 72:12-13 For he shall deliver the needy when he crieth; the poor also, and him that hath no helper. 13 He shall spare the poor and needy, and shall save the souls of the needy.

Psalms 107:41 Yet setteth he the poor on high from affliction, and maketh him families like a flock.

Psalms 69:33 For the LORD heareth the poor, and despiseth not his prisoners.

Jeremiah 20:13 Sing unto the LORD, praise ye the LORD: for he hath delivered the soul of the poor from the hand of evildoers.

Psalms 102:17 He will regard the prayer of the destitute, and not despise their prayer.

Psalms 113:7 He raiseth up the poor out of the dust, and lifteth the needy out of the dunghill.

Psalms 132:15 I will abundantly bless her provision: I will satisfy her poor with bread.

Psalms 68:10 Thy congregation hath dwelt therein: thou, O God, hast prepared of thy goodness for the poor.

Praise and Thanks

Psalms 6:5 For in death there is no remembrance of thee: in the grave who shall give thee thanks?

Psalms 33:1 Rejoice in the LORD, O ye righteous: for praise is comely for the upright.

Psalms 50:23 Whoso offereth praise glorifieth me: and to him that ordereth his conversation aright will I show the salvation of God.

Psalms 148:14a **[Study Psalms 145-150, use them in your prayer life; they can be very edifying!]**
He also exalteth the horn of his people, the praise of all his saints…"

Psalms 149:1 Praise ye the LORD. Sing unto the LORD a new song, and his praise in the congregation of saints.

Isaiah 25:1O LORD, thou art my God; I will exalt thee, I will praise thy name; for thou hast done wonderful things; thy counsels of old are faithfulness and truth.

Isaiah 38:18 For the grave cannot praise thee, death can not celebrate thee: they that go down into the pit cannot hope for thy truth.

Isaiah 43:21 This people have I formed for myself; they shall show forth my praise.

Isaiah 61:3b "… to give unto them beauty for ashes, the oil of joy for mourning, the garment of praise for the spirit of heaviness; … "

Philippians 4:6 Be careful for nothing; but in every thing by prayer and supplication with thanksgiving let your requests be made known unto God.

1 Thessalonians 5:18 In every thing give thanks: for this is the will of God in Christ Jesus concerning you.

Hebrews 13:15 By him therefore let us offer the sacrifice of praise to God continually, that is, the fruit of our lips giving thanks to his name.

1 Peter 2:9 But ye are a chosen generation, a royal priesthood, an holy nation, a peculiar people; that ye should show forth the praises of him who hath called you out of darkness into his marvellous light.

Prayer

Matthew 7:7-8
Ask, and it shall be given you; seek, and ye shall find; knock, and it shall be opened unto you: [8] For every one that asketh receiveth; and he that seeketh findeth; and to him that knocketh it shall be opened.

Matthew 21:22 And all things, whatsoever ye shall ask in prayer, believing, ye shall receive.

Isaiah 30:19 For the people shall dwell in Zion at Jerusalem: thou shalt weep no more: he will be very gracious unto thee at the voice of thy cry; when he shall hear it, he will answer thee.

1 John 5:14-15 And this is the confidence that we have in him, that, if we ask any thing according to his will, he heareth us: And if we know that he hear us, whatsoever we ask, we know that we have the petitions that we desired of him.

Jeremiah 29:12 Then shall ye call upon me, and ye shall go and pray unto me, and I will hearken unto you.

Isaiah 65:24 And it shall come to pass, that before they call, I will answer; and while they are yet speaking, I will hear.

Job 22:27 Thou shalt make thy prayer unto him, and he shall hear thee, and thou shalt pay thy vows.

John 16:23-24
And in that day ye shall ask me nothing. Verily, verily, I say unto you, Whatsoever ye shall ask the Father in my name, he will give *it* you. 24 Hitherto have ye asked nothing in my name: ask, and ye shall receive that your joy may be full.

James 5:16 Confess *your* faults one to another, and pray one for another, that you may be healed. The effectual fervent prayer of a righteous man availeth much.

John 14:13-14 And whatsoever ye shall ask in my name, that will I do, that the Father may be glorified in the Son. [14] If ye shall ask any thing in my name, will do *it*

John 15:7 If ye abide in me, and my words abide in you, ye shall ask what ye will and it shall be done unto you.

Matthew 6:6 But thou, when thou prayest, enter into thy closet, and when thou has shut thy door, pray to thy Father which is in secret; and thy Father which seeth in secret shall reward thee openly.

Psalms 50:15 And call upon me in the day of trouble: I will deliver thee, and thou shalt glorify me.

Isaiah 58:9 Then shalt thou call, and the LORD shall answer; thou shalt cry, and h shall say, Here *I am.* If thou take away from the midst of thee the yoke the putting forth of the finger, and speaking vanity.

Proverbs 15:29 The LORD is far from the wicked: but he heareth the prayer of the righteous.

Psalms 91:15 He shall call upon me, and I will answer him: *I will be* with him in trouble; I will deliver him, and honor him.

Psalms 65:2 O thou that hearest prayer, unto thee shall all flesh come.

Matthew 7:11 If ye then, being evil, know how to give good gifts unto your children, how much more shall your Father which is in heaven give good things to them that ask him?

Psalms 34:17 *The righteous* cry, and the LORD heareth, and delivereth them out of all their troubles.

Psalms 55:1 7Evening, and morning, and at noon, will I pray, and cry aloud: and he shall hear my voice.

Psalms 145:18-19 The LORD is nigh unto all them that call upon him, to all that call upon him in truth. [9] He will fulfill the desire of them that fear him: he also will hear their cry, and will save them.

Matthew 6:8 Be not ye therefore like unto them: for your Father knoweth what things ye have need of, before ye ask him.

1 John 3:22 And whatsoever we ask, we receive of him, because we keep his commandments, and do those things that are pleasing in his sight.

Zechariah 13:9
And I will bring the third part through the fire, and will refine them as silver is refined, and will try them as gold is tried: they shall call on my name, and I will hear them: I will say, It *is* my people: and they shall say, The LORD *is* my God.

Jeremiah 33:3 Call unto me, and I will answer thee, and show thee great and mighty things, which thou knowest not.

Mark 11:24 Therefore I say unto you, what things soever ye desire, when ye pray believe that ye receive *them,* and ye shall have *them.*

Pride

Proverbs 16:18 Pride *goeth* before destruction, and an haughty spirit before a fall.

Isaiah 5:21 Woe unto *them that are* wise in their own eyes, and prudent in their own sight!

Proverbs 26:12 Seest thou a man wise in his own conceit? *There is* more hope of a fool than of him.

Job 40:12 Look on every one *that is* proud, *and* bring him low; and tread down the wicked in their place.

Proverbs 21:4 An high look, and a proud heart, *and* the plowing of the wicked, *is* sin.

Psalms 119:21 Thou hast rebuked the proud *that are* cursed, which do err from thy commandments.

Proverbs 28:25-26 He that is of a proud heart stirreth up strife: but he that putteth his trust in the LORD shall be made fat. [26] He that trusteth in his own heart is a fool: but whoso walketh wisely, he shall be delivered.

Proverbs 8:13 The fear of the LORD *is* to hate evil: pride, and arrogancy, and the evil way, and the froward mouth, do I hate.

Luke 16:15 And he said unto them, ye are they which justify yourselves before men; but God knoweth your hearts: for that which is highly esteemed among men is abomination in the sight of God.

Proverbs 27:2 Let another man praise thee, and not thine own mouth; a stranger, any not thine own lips.

2 Corinthians 10:17-18 But he that glorieth, let him glory in the Lord. 18 For not he that commendeth himself is approved, but whom the Lord commendeth.

John 5:44 How can ye believe, which receive honour one of another, and seek not the honor that *cometh from* God only?

Mark 9:35 And he sat down, and called the twelve, and saith unto them, If any man desire to be first, *the same* shall be last of all, and servant of all.

Prisoners

Isaiah 49:25 But thus saith the LORD, Even the captives of the mighty shall be taken away, and the prey of the terrible shall be delivered: for I will contend with him that contendeth with thee, and I will save thy children.

Deuteronomy 30:4 If any of thine be driven out unto the outmost parts of heaven, from thence will the LORD thy God gather thee, and from thence will he fetch thee:

Psalms 69:33 For the LORD heareth the poor, and despiseth not his prisoners.

Psalms 107:14 He brought them out of darkness and the shadow of death, and brake their bands in sunder.

Psalms 146:7 Which executeth judgment for the oppressed: which giveth food to the hungry. The LORD looseth the prisoners:

Psalms 68:6 God setteth the solitary in families: he bringeth out those which are bound with chains: but the rebellious dwell in a dry land.

Protection, God's

Psalms 18:10 And he rode upon a cherub, and did fly: yea, he did fly upon the wings of the wind.

Job 5:22 At destruction and famine thou shalt laugh: neither shalt thou be afraid of the beasts of the earth.

Job 11:18-19 And thou shalt be secure, because there is hope; yea, thou shalt dig about thee, and thou shalt take thy rest in safety. 19 Also thou shalt lie down, and none shall make thee afraid; yea, any shall make suit unto thee.

Psalms 121:8 The LORD shall preserve thee from all evil: he shall preserve thy soul. 8 The LORD shall preserve thy going out and thy coming in from this time forth, and even for evermore.

Proverbs 3:24 When thou liest down, thou shalt not be afraid: yea, thou shalt lie down, and thy sleep shall be sweet.

1 Peter 3:13 And who is he that will harm you, if ye be followers of that which is good?

Deuteronomy 33:12 And of Benjamin he said, the beloved of the LORD shall dwell in safety by him; and the LORD shall cover him all the day long, and he shall dwell between his shoulders.

Psalms 112:7 He shall not be afraid of evil tidings: his heart is fixed, trusting in the LORD.

Psalms 91:9-10 Because thou hast made the LORD, which is my refuge, even the most High, thy habitation; 10 There shall no evil befall thee, neither shall any plague come nigh thy dwelling.

Isaiah 43:1-2 But now thus saith the LORD that created thee, O Jacob, and he that formed thee, O Israel, Fear not: for I have redeemed thee, I have called thee by thy name; thou art mine. 2 When thou passest through the waters, I will be with thee; and through the rivers, they shall not overflow thee: when thou walkest through the fire, thou shalt not be burned; neither shall the flame kindle upon thee.

Ezekiel 34:28 And they shall no more be a prey to the heathen, neither shall the beast of the land devour them; but they shall dwell safely, and none shall make them afraid.

Proverbs 1:33 But whoso hearkeneth unto me shall dwell safely, and shall be quiet from fear of evil.

Psalms 4:8 I will both lay me down in peace, and sleep: for thou, LORD, only makest me dwell in safety.

Psalms 27:1 A Psalm of David. The LORD is my light and my salvation; whom shall I fear? The LORD is the strength of my life; of whom shall I be afraid?

Repentance

Mark 1:15 And saying, the time is fulfilled, and the kingdom of God is at hand: repent ye, and believe the gospel.

Mark 6:12 And they went out, and preached that men should repent.

Psalms 34:18 The LORD is nigh unto them that are of a broken heart; and saveth such as be of a contrite spirit.

Psalms 147:3 He healeth the broken in heart, and bindeth up their wounds.

Job 11:14-15 If iniquity be in thine hand, put it far away, and let not wickedness dwell in thy tabernacles. 15 For then shalt thou lift up thy face without spot; yea, thou shalt be stedfast, and shalt not fear.

Ezekiel 18:21-22
But if the wicked will turn from all his sins that he hath committed, and keep all my statutes, and do that which is lawful and right, he shall surely live, he shall not die. 22 All his transgressions that he hath committed, they shall not be mentioned unto him: in his righteousness that he hath done he shall live.

Luke 5:27-32
And after these things he went forth, and saw a publican, named Levi, sitting at the receipt of custom: and he said unto him, Follow

me. 28 And he left all, rose up, and followed him. 29 And Levi made him a great feast in his own house: and there was a great company of publicans and of others that sat down with them. 30 But their scribes and Pharisees murmured against his disciples, saying, why do ye eat and drink with publicans and sinners? 31 And Jesus answering said unto them, they that are whole need not a physician; but they that are sick. 32 I came not to call the righteous, but sinners to repentance.

Luke 5:31-32 And Jesus answering said unto them, they that are whole need not a physician; but they that are sick. 32 I came not to call the righteous, but sinners to repentance.

Matthew 4:17 From that time Jesus began to preach, and to say, Repent: for the kingdom of heaven is at hand.

Mark 7:20-23
And he said, that which cometh out of the man, that defileth the man. 21 For from within, out of the heart of men, proceed evil thoughts, adulteries, fornications, murders, 22 Thefts, covetousness, wickedness, deceit, lasciviousness, an evil eye, blasphemy, pride, foolishness: 23 All these evil things come from within, and defile the man.

Jeremiah 4:3-4
For thus saith the LORD to the men of Judah and Jerusalem, Break up your fallow ground, and sow not among thorns. 4 Circumcise yourselves to the LORD, and take away the foreskins of your heart, ye men of Judah and inhabitants of Jerusalem: lest my fury come forth like fire, and burn that none can quench it, because of the evil of your doings.

Joel 2:12-13
Therefore also now, saith the LORD, turn ye even to me with all your heart, and with fasting, and with weeping, and with mourning: 13 And rend your heart, and not your garments, and turn unto the

LORD your God: for he is gracious and merciful, slow to anger, and of great kindness, and repenteth him of the evil.

2 Corinthians 7:8-11
For though I made you sorry with a letter, I do not repent, though I did repent: for I perceive that the same epistle hath made you sorry, though it were but for a season. 9 Now I rejoice, not that ye were made sorry, but that ye sorrowed to repentance: for ye were made sorry after a godly manner, that ye might receive damage by us in nothing. 10 For godly sorrow worketh repentance to salvation not to be repented of: but the sorrow of the world worketh death. 11 For behold this selfsame thing, that ye sorrowed after a godly sort, what carefulness it wrought in you, yea, what clearing of yourselves, yea, what indignation, yea, what fear, yea, what vehement desire, yea, what zeal, yea, what revenge! In all things ye have approved yourselves to be clear in this matter.

2 Corinthians 7:10-11
For godly sorrow worketh repentance to salvation not to be repented of: but the sorrow of the world worketh death. 11 For behold this selfsame thing, that ye sorrowed after a godly sort, what carefulness it wrought in you, yea, what clearing of yourselves, yea, what indignation, yea, what fear, yea, what vehement desire, yea, what zeal, yea, what revenge! In all things ye have approved yourselves to be clear in this matter.

Luke 15:7 I say unto you, that likewise joy shall be in heaven over one sinner that repenteth, more than over ninety and nine just persons, which need no repentance.

Isaiah 55:6-7
Seek ye the LORD while he may be found, call ye upon him while he is near: 7 Let the wicked forsake his way, and the unrighteous man his thoughts: and let him return unto the LORD, and he will have mercy upon him; and to our God, for he will abundantly pardon.

Ezekiel 14:1-11
Then came certain of the elders of Israel unto me, and sat before me. 2 And the word of the LORD came unto me, saying, 3 Son of man, these men have set up their idols in their heart, and put the stumblingblock of their iniquity before their face: should I be inquired of at all by them? 4 Therefore speak unto them, and say unto them, Thus saith the Lord GOD; Every man of the house of Israel that setteth up his idols in his heart, and putteth the stumblingblock of his iniquity before his face, and cometh to the prophet; I the LORD will answer him that cometh according to the multitude of his idols; 5 That I may take the house of Israel in their own heart, because they are all estranged from me through their idols. 6 Therefore say unto the house of Israel, Thus saith the Lord GOD; Repent, and turn yourselves from your idols; and turn away your faces from all your abominations. 7 For every one of the house of Israel, or of the stranger that sojourneth in Israel, which separateth himself from me, and setteth up his idols in his heart, and putteth the stumblingblock of his iniquity before his face, and cometh to a prophet to inquire of him concerning me; I the LORD will answer him by myself: 8 And I will set my face against that man, and will make him a sign and a proverb, and I will cut him off from the midst of my people; and ye shall know that I am the LORD. 9 And if the prophet be deceived when he hath spoken a thing, I the LORD have deceived that prophet, and I will stretch out my hand upon him, and will destroy him from the midst of my people Israel. 10 And they shall bear the punishment of their iniquity: the punishment of the prophet shall be even as the punishment of him that seeketh unto him; 11 That the house of Israel may go no more astray from me, neither be polluted any more with all their transgressions; but that they may be my people, and I may be their God, saith the Lord GOD.

Ezekiel 14:6 Therefore say unto the house of Israel, Thus saith the Lord GOD; Repent, and turn yourselves from your idols; and turn away your faces from all your abominations.

Ezekiel 18:21-22
But if the wicked will turn from all his sins that he hath committed, and keep all my statutes, and do that which is lawful and right, he shall surely live, he shall not die. 22 All his transgressions that he hath committed, they shall not be mentioned unto him: in his righteousness that he hath done he shall live.

Ezekiel 18:23 Have I any pleasure at all that the wicked should die? Saith the Lord GOD: and not that he should return from his ways, and live?

Ezekiel 18:30-32
Therefore I will judge you, O house of Israel, every one according to his ways, saith the Lord GOD. Repent, and turn yourselves from all your transgressions; so iniquity shall not be your ruin. 31 Cast away from you all your transgressions, whereby ye have transgressed; and make you a new heart and a new spirit: for why will ye die, O house of Israel? 32 For I have no pleasure in the death of him that dieth, saith the Lord GOD: wherefore turn yourselves, and live ye.

Matthew 11:20-24
Then began he to upbraid the cities wherein most of his mighty works were done, because they repented not: 21 Woe unto thee, Chorazin. Woe unto thee, Bethsaida! for if the mighty works, which were done in you, had been done in Tyre and Sidon, they would have repented long ago in sackcloth and ashes.22 But I say unto you, It shall be more tolerable for Tyre and Sidon at the day of judgment, than for you. 23 And thou, Capernaum, which art exalted unto heaven, shalt be brought down to hell: for if the mighty works, which have been done in thee, had been done in Sodom, it would have remained until this day. 24 But I say unto you, that it shall be more tolerable for the land of Sodom in the day of judgment, than for thee.

Romans 2:4 Or despisest thou the riches of his goodness and forbearance and longsuffering; not knowing that the goodness of God leadeth thee to repentance?

Romans 2:5-11
But after thy hardness and impenitent heart treasurest up unto thyself wrath against the day of wrath and revelation of the righteous judgment of God; 6 Who will render to every man according to his deeds: 7 To them who by patient continuance in well doing seek for glory and honour and immortality, eternal life: 8 But unto them that are contentious, and do not obey the truth, but obey unrighteousness, indignation and wrath, 9 Tribulation and anguish, upon every soul of man that doeth evil, of the Jew first, and also of the Gentile; 10 But glory, honour, and peace, to every man that worketh good, to the Jew first, and also to the Gentile: 11 For there is no respect of persons with God.

Romans 2:5-6 But after thy hardness and impenitent heart treasurest up unto thyself wrath against the day of wrath and revelation of the righteous judgment of God; 6 Who will render to every man according to his deeds:

Righteousness

Psalms 84:11 For the LORD God is a sun and shield: the LORD will give grace and glory: no good thing will he withhold from them that walk uprightly.

Psalms 34:10 The young lions do lack, and suffer hunger: but they that seek the LORD shall not want any good thing.

Proverbs 10:24 The fear of the wicked, it shall come upon him: but the desire of the righteous shall be granted

Proverbs 13:21 Evil pursueth sinners: but to the righteous good shall be repayed.

Proverbs 12:2 A good man obtaineth favour of the LORD: but a man of wicked devices will he condemn.

Matthew 6:33 But seek ye first the kingdom of God, and his righteousness; and all these things shall be added unto you.

Proverbs 11:28 He that trusteth in his riches shall fall: but the righteous shall flourish as a branch.

Psalms 58:11 So that a man shall say, verily there is a reward for the righteous: verily he is a God that judgeth in the earth.

Psalms 5:12 For thou, LORD, wilt bless the righteous; with favour wilt thou compass him as with a shield.

Psalms 3:8 Salvation belongeth unto the LORD: thy blessing is upon thy people. Selah.

1 Corinthians 3:22-23 Whether Paul, or Apollos, or Cephas, or the world, or life, or death, or things present, or things to come; all are yours; 23 And ye are Christ's; and Christ is God's.

Romans 6:32 He that spared not his own Son, but delivered him up for us all, how shall he not with him also freely give us all things?

Isaiah 3:10 Say ye to the righteous, that it shall be well with him: for they shall eat the fruit of their doings.

Psalms 23:6 Surely goodness and mercy shall follow me all the days of my life: and I will dwell in the house of the LORD for ever.

Salvation

John 3:16 For God so loved the world, that he gave his only begotten Son, that whosoever believeth in him should not perish, but have everlasting life.

John 3:17 For God sent not his Son into the world to condemn the world; but that the world through him might be saved.

Acts 4:12 Neither is there salvation in any other: for there is none other name under heaven given among men, whereby we must be saved.

John 3:3 Jesus answered and said unto him, Verily, verily, I say unto thee, Except a man be born again, he cannot see the kingdom of God.

John 3:4-7
Nicodemus saith unto him, How can a man be born when he is old? Can he enter the second time into his mother's womb, and be born? [5] Jesus answered, Verily, verily, I say unto thee, except a man be born of water and of the Spirit, he cannot enter into the kingdom of God. [6] That which is born of the flesh is flesh; and that which is born of the Spirit is spirit. Marvel not that I said unto thee, Ye must he born again.

Romans 1:16 For I am not ashamed of the gospel of Christ: for it is the power of God unto salvation to every one that believeth; to the Jew first, and also to the Greek.

Romans 10:9-10
That if thou shalt confess with thy mouth the Lord Jesus, and shalt believe in thine heart that God hath raised him from the dead, thou shalt be saved. 10 For with the heart man believeth unto righteousness; and with the mouth confession is made unto salvation.

Romans 10:13 For whosoever shall call upon the name of the Lord shall be saved.

Titus 2:11 For the grace of God that bringeth salvation bath appeared to all men.

Hebrews 1:14 Are they not all ministering spirits, sent forth to minister for them who shall be heirs of salvation?

2 Corinthians 5:17 Therefore if any man *be* in Christ, *he is* a new creature: old things are passed away; behold, all things are become new.

2 Corinthians 5:21 For he hath made him *to be* sin for us, who knew no sin; that we might be made the righteousness of God in him.

Ephesians 2:1 And you *hath he quickened,* who were dead in trespasses and sins.

1Timothy 2:3-4 For this is good and acceptable in the sight of God our Saviour; who will have all men to be saved, and to come unto the knowledge of the, truth.

1 John 2:1-2 My little children, these things write I unto you, that ye sin not. And if any man sin, we have an advocate with the Father,

Jesus Christ the righteous: 2 And he is the propitiation for our sins: and not for our only, but also for *the sins of* the whole world.

Colossians 2:13 And you, being dead in your sins and the uncircumcision of your fleshhath he quickened together with him, having forgiven you all trespasses.

1Timothy 4:9-10 This *is* a faithful saying and worthy of all acceptation. [10] For therefore we both labour and suffer reproach, because we trust in the living God, who is the Saviour of all men, specially of those that believe.

Romans 5:15
But not as the offence, so also *is* the free gift. For if through the offence of one many be dead, much more the grace of God, and the gift by grace, *which is* by one man, Jesus Christ, hath abounded unto many.

Titus 3:4-6
But after that the kindness and love of God our Saviour toward man appeared, not by works of righteousness which we have done, but according to his mercy he saved us, by the washing of regeneration, and renewing of the Holy Ghost; [6] Which he shed on us abundantly through Jesus Christ our Saviour.

Prayer That Saves

Dear Heavenly Father, I come unto thee in the name of your Son Jesus Christ whom I believe and receive as the Son of the true and living God, and the Savior of the world. I am a sinner, and have need of your salvation. Therefore, I come in the name of Jesus Christ, confessing and repenting of my sins, and asking for your forgiveness. Purge me, cleanse me, and make me whole. For I believe in my heart and confess with my mouth that Jesus Christ is Lord and Savior. I believe in my heart and confess with my mouth the death, burial, and resurrection of Jesus Christ according to the Holy Scriptures. Now Lord, come into my heart, fill me with you Holy Spirit, and make me alive unto Jesus Christ. I thank you Lord that you have saved me and that I am being filled with your Holy Spirit. Amen.

Seeking God

2 Chronicles 15:2
And he went out to meet Asa, and said unto him, Hear ye me, Asa, and all Judah and Benjamin; The LORD is with you, while ye be with him; and if ye seek him, he will be found of you; but if ye forsake him, he will forsake you.

Hosea 10:12 Sow to yourselves in righteousness, reap in mercy; break up your fallow ground: for it is time to seek the LORD, till he come and rain righteousness upon you.

Hebrews 11:6 But without faith it is impossible to please him: for he that cometh to God must believe that he is, and that he is a rewarder of them that diligently seek him.

Acts 17:27 That they should seek the Lord, if haply they might feel after him, and find him, though he be not far from every one of us:

Lamentations 3:25 The LORD is good unto them that wait for him, to the soul that seeketh him.

Amos 5:4 For thus saith the LORD unto the house of Israel, Seek ye me, and ye shall live:

Jeremiah 29:13 And ye shall seek me, and find me, when ye shall search for me with all your heart.

Deuteronomy 4:29 But if from thence thou shalt seek the LORD thy God, thou shalt find him, if thou seek him with all thy heart and with all thy soul.

Ezra 8:22
For I was ashamed to require of the king a band of soldiers and horsemen to help us against the enemy in the way: because we had spoken unto the king, saying, The hand of our God is upon all them for good that seek him; but his power and his wrath is against all them that forsake him.

1 Chronicles 28:9
And thou, Solomon my son, know thou the God of thy father, and serve him with a perfect heart and with a willing mind: for the LORD searcheth all hearts, and understandeth all the imaginations of the thoughts: if thou seek him, he will be found of thee; but if thou forsake him, he will cast thee off for ever.

Job 8:5-6 If thou wouldest seek unto God betimes, and make thy supplication to the Almighty; 6 If thou wert pure and upright; surely now he would awake for thee, and make the habitation of thy righteousness prosperous.

Psalms 9:10 And they that know thy name will put their trust in thee: for thou, LORD, hast not forsaken them that seek thee.

Self-denial

Matthew 16:24-26
Then said Jesus unto his disciples, If any man will come after me, let him deny himself, and take up his cross, and follow me. 25 For whosoever will save his life shall lose it: and whosoever will lose his life for my sake shall find it. 26 For what is a man profited, if he shall gain the whole world, and lose his own soul? Or what shall a man give in exchange for his soul?

Romans 8:12-13 Therefore, brethren, we are debtors, not to the flesh, to live after the flesh. 13 For if ye live after the flesh, ye shall die: but if ye through the Spirit do mortify the deeds of the body, ye shall live.

Galatians 5:24 And they that are Christ's have crucified the flesh with the affections and lusts.

Titus 2:11-12 For the grace of God that bringeth salvation hath appeared to all men, 12 Teaching us that, denying ungodliness and worldly lusts, we should live soberly, righteously, and godly, in this present world.

Luke 18:29-30
And he said unto them, Verily I say unto you, There is no man that hath left house, or parents, or brethren, or wife, or children, for the kingdom of God's sake, 30 Who shall not receive manifold more in this present time, and in the world to come life everlasting.

Matthew 5:39-41
But I say unto you, that ye resist not evil: but whosoever shall smite
thee on thy right cheek, turn to him the other also. 40 And if any
man will sue thee at the law, and take away thy coat, let him have
thy cloak also. 41 And whosoever shall compel thee to go a mile, go
with him twain.

Self-righteousness

Job 33:8-9 Surely thou hast spoken in mine hearing, and I have heard the voice of thy words, saying, 9 I am clean without transgression, I am innocent; neither is there iniquity in me.

Job 35:2 Thinkest thou this to be right, that thou saidst, My righteousness is more than God's?

Isaiah 5:21 Woe unto them that are wise in their own eyes, and prudent in their own sight!

Job 35:13 Surely God will not hear vanity, neither will the Almighty regard it.

Psalms 26:12 My foot standeth in an even place: in the congregations will I bless the LORD.

Galatians 6:3 For if a man think himself to be something, when he is nothing, he deceiveth himself.

2 Corinthians 10:17-18 But he that glorieth, let him glory in the Lord.18 For not he that commendeth himself is approved, but whom the Lord commendeth.

John 9:41 Jesus said unto them, If ye were blind, ye should have no sin: but now ye say, We see; therefore your sin remaineth.

Isaiah 64:6 But we are all as an unclean thing, and all our righteousnesses are as filthy rags; and we all do fade as a leaf; and our iniquities, like the wind, have taken us away.

Proverbs 28:25-26
He that is of a proud heart stirreth up strife: but he that putteth his trust in the LORD shall be made fat. 26 He that trusteth in his own heart is a fool: but whoso walketh wisely, he shall be delivered.

Luke 16:15 And he said unto them, Ye are they which justify yourselves before men; but God knoweth your hearts: for that which is highly esteemed among men is abomination in the sight of God.

Proverbs 27:2 Let another man praise thee, and not thine own mouth; a stranger, and not thine own lips.

Sexual Sins

1 Corinthians 6:13 Meats for the belly, and the belly for meats: but God shall destroy both it and them. Now the body is not for fornication, but for the Lord; and the Lord for the body.

1 Corinthians 6:18-20 Flee fornication. Every sin that a man doeth is without the body; but he that committeth fornication sinneth against his own body. What' know ye not that your body is the temple of the Holy Ghost *which is in* you, which ye have of God, and ye are not your own? [20] For ye an bought with a price: therefore glorify God in your body, and in you spirit, which are God's.

1 Corinthians 7:1 Now concerning the things whereof ye wrote unto me: *It* is good for man not to touch a woman.

1 Corinthians 7:8-9 I say therefore to the unmarried and widows, It is good for them if the: abide even as I. [9] But if they cannot contain, let them marry: for it i better to marry than to burn.

1 Corinthians 7:37 Nevertheless he that standeth stedfast in his heart, having no necessity but hath power over his own will, and hath so decreed in his heart that he will keep his virgin, doeth well.

1 Corinthians 10:13
There hath no temptation taken you but such as is common to man: but God *is* faithful, who will not suffer you to be tempted above that ye are able; but will with the temptation also make a way to escape, that y may be able to bear *it*.

Revelation 14:4
These are they which were not defiled with women. For they are virgins. These are they which follow the Lamb whithersoever he goeth.Grace, that we may obtain mercy. And find grace to help in time of need. These were redeemed from among men, being the firstfruits unto God and to the Lamb.

1 Thessalonians 4:3 For this is the will of God, even your sanctification, that ye should abstain from fornication.

Hebrews 13:4 Marriage is honourable in all, and the bed undefiled: but whoremongers and adulterers God will judge.

1 Corinthians 6:15 Know ye not that your bodies are the members of Christ? Shall I then take the members of Christ, and make them the members of an harlot? God forbid.

Proverbs 31:10 Who can find a virtuous woman? For her price is far above rubies.

Hebrews 2:18 For in that he himself bath suffered being tempted, he is able to succour them that are tempted.

2 Peter 2:9 The Lord knoweth how to deliver the godly out of Temptations, and to reserve the unjust unto the day of judgment to be punished.

James 1:12 Blessed is the man that endureth temptation: for when he is tried, he shall receive the crown of life, which the Lord bath promised to them that love him.

Hebrews 4:15-16 For we have not an high priest which cannot be touched with the feeling of our infirmities; but was in all points tempted like as we are, yet without sin. 16 Let us therefore come boldly unto the throne of grace, that we may obtain mercy, and find grace to help in time of need.

Shame

Romans 10:11 For the scripture saith, Whosoever believeth on him shall not be ashamed.

Psalms 119:6 Then shall I not be ashamed, when I have respect unto all thy commandments.

Romans 5:5 And hope maketh not ashamed; because the love of God is shed abroad in our hearts by the Holy Ghost which is given unto us.

2 Timothy 1:12 For the which cause I also suffer these things: nevertheless I am not ashamed: for I know whom I have believed, and am persuaded that he is able to keep that which I have committed unto him against that day.

Romans 9:33 As it is written, Behold, I lay in Sion a stumblingstone and rock of offence: and whosoever believeth on him shall not be ashamed.

2 Timothy 2:15 Study to show thyself approved unto God, a workman that needeth not to be ashamed, rightly dividing the word of truth.

1 Peter 4:16 Yet if any man suffer as a Christian, let him not be ashamed; but let him glorify God on this behalf.

Psalms 119:80 Let my heart be sound in thy statutes; that I be not ashamed.

Sickness

James 5:14-16
Is any sick among you? Let him call for the elders of the church; and let them pray over him, anointing him with oil in the name of the Lord: 15 And the prayer of faith shall save the sick, and the Lord shall raise him up; and if he have committed sins, they shall be forgiven him. 16 Confess your faults one to another, and pray one for another, that ye may be healed. The effectual fervent prayer of a righteous man availeth much.

Matthew 9:28-30
And when he was come into the house, the blind men came to him: and Jesus saith unto them, Believe ye that I am able to do this? They said unto him, Yea, Lord. 29 Then touched he their eyes, saying, According to your faith be it unto you. 30 And their eyes were opened; and Jesus straitly charged them, saying, See that no man know it.

Jeremiah 17:14 Heal me, O LORD, and I shall be healed; save me, and I shall be saved: for thou art my praise.

Matthew 9:6-7 But that ye may know that the Son of man hath power on earth to forgive sins, (then saith he to the sick of the palsy,) Arise, take up thy bed, and go unto thine house. 7 And he arose, and departed to his house.

Matthew 4:23-24

And Jesus went about all Galilee, teaching in their synagogues, and preaching the gospel of the kingdom, and healing all manner of sickness and all manner of disease among the people 24 And his fame went throughout all Syria: and they brought unto him all sick people that were taken with divers diseases and torments, and those which were possessed with devils, and those which were lunatic, and those that had the palsy; and he healed them.

Jeremiah 30:17 For I will restore health unto thee, and I will heal thee of thy wounds, saith the LORD; because they called thee an Outcast, saying, this is Zion, whom no man seeketh after.

Exodus 23:25 And ye shall serve the LORD your God, and he shall bless thy bread, and thy water; and I will take sickness away from the midst of thee.

1 Peter 2:24 Who his own self bare our sins in his own body on the tree that we, being dead to sins, should live unto righteousness: by whose stripes ye were healed.

Isaiah 53:5 But he was wounded for our transgressions, he was bruised for our iniquities: the chastisement of our peace was upon him; and with his stripes we are healed.

Sin, freedom from

Ezekiel 36:25-26
Then will I sprinkle clean water upon you, and ye shall be clean: from all your filthiness, and from all your idols, will I cleanse you. 26 A new heart also will I give you, and a new spirit will I put within you: and I will take away the stony heart out of your flesh, and I will give you an heart of flesh.

Acts 10:43 To him give all the prophets' witness, that through his name whosoever, believeth in him shall receive remission of sins.

Romans 6:6-7 Knowing this, that our old man is crucified with him, that the body of sin might be destroyed, that henceforth we should not serve sin. 7 For he that is dead is freed from sin.

2 Corinthians 5:17 Therefore if any man be in Christ, he is a new creature: old things are passed away; behold, all things are become new.

Romans 6:1-2 What shall we say then? Shall we continue in sin, that grace may abound? 2 God forbid. How shall we, that are dead to sin, live any longer therein?

Romans 6:11 Likewise reckon ye also yourselves to be dead indeed unto sin, but alive unto God through Jesus Christ our Lord.

Romans 6:14 For sin shall not have dominion over you: for ye are not under the law, but under grace.

Matthew 1:21 And she shall bring forth a son, and thou shalt call his name JESUS: for he shall save his people from their sins.

Acts 13:38 Be it known unto you therefore, men and brethren, that through this man is preached unto you the forgiveness of sins:

1 John3:5 And ye know that he was manifested to take away our sins; and in him is no sin.

1 John 2:1-2
My little children, these things write I unto you, that ye sin not. And if any man sin, we have an advocate with the Father, Jesus Christ the righteous: 2 And he is the propitiation for our sins: and not for ours only, but also for the sins of the whole world.

1 Peter 2:24 Who his own self bare our sins in his own body on the tree, that we, being dead to sins, should live unto righteousness: by whose stripes ye were healed.

1 Timothy 1:15
This is a faithful saying, and worthy of all acceptation, that Christ Jesus came into the world to save sinners; of whom I am chief.

Isaiah 53:5-6 But he was wounded for our transgressions, he was bruised for our iniquities: the chastisement of our peace was upon him; and with his stripes we are healed. 6 All we like sheep have gone astray; we have turned every one to his own way; and the LORD hath laid on him the iniquity of us all.

John 1:29 The next day John seeth Jesus coming unto him, and saith, Behold the Lamb of God, which taketh away the sin of the world.

Ephesians 1:7 In whom we have redemption through his blood, the forgiveness of sins, according to the riches of his grace.

Galatians 1:4 Who gave himself for our sins, that he might deliver us from this present evil world, according to the will of God and our Father:
Hebrews 9:28 So Christ was once offered to bear the sins of many; and unto them that look for him shall he appear the second time without sin unto salvation.

Hebrews 10:14 For by one offering he hath perfected for ever them that are sanctified.

Slander and reproach

Matthew 5:11-12
Blessed are ye, when men shall revile you, and persecute you, and shall say all manner of evil against you falsely, for my sake. 12
Rejoice, and be exceeding glad: for great is your reward in heaven: for so persecuted they the prophets which were before you.

Peter 4:14 If ye be reproached for the name of Christ, happy are ye; for the spirit of glory and of God resteth upon you: on their part he is evil spoken of, but on your part he is glorified.

Psalms 57:3 He shall send from heaven, and save me from the reproach of him that would swallow me up. Selah. God shall send forth his mercy and his truth.

Psalms 31:20 Thou shalt hide them in the secret of thy presence from the pride of man: thou shalt keep them secretly in a pavilion from the strife of tongues.

Job 5:21 Thou shalt be hid from the scourge of the tongue: neither shalt thou be afraid of destruction when it cometh.

Psalms 37:6 And he shall bring forth thy righteousness as the light, and thy judgment as the noonday.

Success

Proverbs 15:6 In the house of the righteous is much treasure: but in the revenues of the wicked is trouble.

Proverbs 22:4 By humility and the fear of the LORD are riches, and honour, and life.

Deuteronomy 30:9 And the LORD thy God will make thee plenteous in every work of thine hand, in the fruit of thy body, and in the fruit of thy cattle, and in the fruit of thy land, for good: for the LORD will again rejoice over thee for good, as he rejoiced over thy fathers:

Isaiah 30:23 Then shall he give the rain of thy seed, that thou shalt sow the ground withal; and bread of the increase of the earth, and it shall be fat and plenteous: in that day shall thy cattle feed in large pastures.

Ecclesiastes 3:13 And also that every man should eat and drink, and enjoy the good of all his labour, it is the gift of God.

Deuteronomy 28:11-13
And the LORD shall make thee plenteous in goods, in the fruit of thy body, and in the fruit of thy cattle, and in the fruit of thy ground, in the land which the LORD sware unto thy fathers to give thee.12 The LORD shall open unto thee his good treasure, the heaven to give the rain unto thy land in his season, and to bless all the work of

thine hand: and thou shalt lend unto many nations, and thou shalt not borrow. 13 And the LORD shall make thee the head, and not the tail; and thou shalt be above only, and thou shalt not be beneath; if that thou hearken unto the commandments of the LORD thy God, which I command thee this day, to observe and to do them:

Ecclesiastes 5:19 Every man also to whom God hath given riches and wealth, and hath given him power to eat thereof, and to take his portion, and to rejoice in his labour; this is the gift of God.

Job 22:28 Thou shalt also decree a thing, and it shall be established unto thee: and the light shall shine upon thy ways.

Proverbs 8:18-19 Riches and honour are with me; yea, durable riches and righteousness. 19 My fruit is better than gold, yea, than fine gold; and my revenue than choice silver.

Psalms 112:3 Wealth and riches shall be in his house: and his righteousness endureth for ever.

Job 22:24-25 Then shalt thou lay up gold as dust, and the gold of Ophir as the stones of the brooks. 25 Yea, the Almighty shall be thy defence, and thou shalt have plenty of silver.

Deuteronomy 11:15 And I will send grass in thy fields for thy cattle, that thou mayest eat and be full.

Psalms 128:2 For thou shalt eat the labour of thine hands: happy shalt thou be, and it shall be well with thee.

Isaiah 65:21-23
And they shall build houses, and inhabit them; and they shall plant vineyards, and eat the fruit of them. 22 They shall not build, and another inhabit; they shall not plant, and another eat: for as the days of a tree are the days of my people, and mine elect shall long enjoy the work of their hands. 23 They shall not labour in vain, nor bring

forth for trouble; for they are the seed of the blessed of the LORD, and their offspring with them.

Deuteronomy 28:2-6
And all these blessings shall come on thee, and overtake thee, if thou shalt hearken unto the voice of the LORD thy God. 28:3 Blessed shalt thou be in the city, and blessed shalt thou be in the field. 4 Blessed shall be the fruit of thy body, and the fruit of thy ground, and the fruit of thy cattle, the increase of thy kine, and the flocks of thy sheep. 5 Blessed shall be thy basket and thy store.6 Blessed shalt thou be when thou comest in, and blessed shalt thou be when thou goest out.

Tithing

Genesis 14:20 And blessed be the most high God, which hath delivered thine enemies into thy hand. And he gave him tithes of all.

Genesis 28:22 And this stone, which I have set for a pillar, shall be God's house: and of all that thou shalt give me I will surely give the tenth unto thee.

Leviticus 27:30-33
And all the tithe of the land, whether of the seed of the land, or of the fruit of the tree, is the LORD'S: it is holy unto the LORD. And all the tithe of the land, whether of the seed of the land, or of the fruit of the tree, is the LORD'S: it is holy unto the LORD. 31 And if a man will at all redeem ought of his tithes, he shall add thereto the fifth part thereof. 32 And concerning the tithe of the herd, or of the flock, even of whatsoever passeth under the rod, the tenth shall be holy unto the LORD. 33 He shall not search whether it be good or bad, neither shall he change it: and if he change it at all, then both it and the change thereof shall be holy; it shall not be redeemed. e 27:31 And if a man will at all redeem ought of his tithes, he shall add thereto the fifth part thereof. 32 And concerning the tithe of the herd, or of the flock, even of whatsoever passeth under the rod, the tenth shall be holy unto the LORD. 33 He shall not search whether it be good or bad, neither shall he change it: and if he change it at all, then both it and the change thereof shall be holy; it shall not be redeemed.

Numbers 18:26 Thus speak unto the Levites, and say unto them, When ye take of the children of Israel the tithes which I have given you from them for your inheritance, then ye shall offer up an heave offering of it for the LORD, even a tenth part of the tithe.

Numbers 18:28-29
Thus ye also shall offer an heave offering unto the LORD of all your tithes, which ye receive of the children of Israel; and ye shall give thereof the LORD'S heave offering to Aaron the priest. 29 Out of all your gifts ye shall offer every heave offering of the LORD, of all the best thereof, even the hallowed part thereof out of it.

Deuteronomy 12:6-7
And thither ye shall bring your burnt offerings, and your sacrifices, and your tithes, and heave offerings of your hand, and your vows, and your freewill offerings, and the firstlings of your herds and of your flocks: 7 And there ye shall eat before the LORD your God, and ye shall rejoice in all that ye put your hand unto, ye and your households, wherein the LORD thy God hath blessed thee.

Deuteronomy 12:11 Then there shall be a place which the LORD your God shall choose to cause his name to dwell there; thither shall ye bring all that I command you; your burnt offerings, and your sacrifices, your tithes, and the heave offering of your hand, and all your choice vows which ye vow unto the LORD:

Deuteronomy 12:17 Thou mayest not eat within thy gates the tithe of thy corn, or of thy wine, or of thy oil, or the firstlings of thy herds or of thy flock, nor any of thy vows which thou vowest, nor thy freewill offerings, or heave offering of thine hand:

Deuteronomy 14:22-29
Thou shalt truly tithe all the increase of thy seed, that the field bringeth forth year by year. 23 And thou shalt eat before the LORD thy God, in the place which he shall choose to place his name there,

the tithe of thy corn, of thy wine, and of thine oil, and the firstlings of thy herds and of thy flocks; that thou mayest learn to fear the LORD thy God always. 24 And if the way be too long for thee, so that thou art not able to carry it; or if the place be too far from thee, which the LORD thy God shall choose to set his name there, when the LORD thy God hath blessed thee: :25 Then shalt thou turn it into money, and bind up the money in thine hand, and shalt go unto the place which the LORD thy God shall choose: 26 And thou shalt bestow that money for whatsoever thy soul lusteth after, for oxen, or for sheep, or for wine, or for strong drink, or for whatsoever thy soul desireth: and thou shalt eat there before the LORD thy God, and thou shalt rejoice, thou, and thine household, 27 And the Levite that is within thy gates; thou shalt not forsake him; for he hath no part nor inheritance with thee. 28 At the end of three years thou shalt bring forth all the tithe of thine increase the same year, and shalt lay it up within thy gates: 29 And the Levite, (because he hath no part nor inheritance with thee,) and the stranger, and the fatherless, and the widow, which are within thy gates, shall come, and shall eat and be satisfied; that the LORD thy God may bless thee in all the work of thine hand which thou doest.

Deuteronomy 26:10-13
And now, behold, I have brought the firstfruits of the land, which thou, O LORD, hast given me. And thou shalt set it before the LORD thy God, and worship before the LORD thy God: 11 And thou shalt rejoice in every good thing which the LORD thy God hath given unto thee, and unto thine house, thou, and the Levite, and the stranger that is among you. 12 When thou hast made an end of tithing all the tithes of thine increase the third year, which is the year of tithing, and hast given it unto the Levite, the stranger, the fatherless, and the widow, that they may eat within thy gates, and be filled; 13 Then thou shalt say before the LORD thy God, I have brought away the hallowed things out of mine house, and also have given them unto the Levite, and unto the stranger, to the fatherless, and to the widow, according to all thy commandments which thou

hast commanded me: I have not transgressed thy commandments, neither have I forgotten them:

Nehemiah 10:37-39
And that we should bring the firstfruits of our dough, and our offerings, and the fruit of all manner of trees, of wine and of oil, unto the priests, to the chambers of the house of our God; and the tithes of our ground unto the Levites, that the same Levites might have the tithes in all the cities of our tillage. 38 And the priest the son of Aaron shall be with the Levites, when the Levites take tithes: and the Levites shall bring up the tithe of the tithes unto the house of our God, to the chambers, into the treasure house. 39 For the children of Israel and the children of Levi shall bring the offering of the corn, of the new wine, and the oil, unto the chambers, where are the vessels of the sanctuary, and the priests that minister, and the porters, and the singers: and we will not forsake the house of our God.

Nehemiah 12:44
And at that time were some appointed over the chambers for the treasures, for the offerings, for the firstfruits, and for the tithes, to gather into them out of the fields of the cities the portions of the law
for the priests and Levites: for Judah rejoiced for the priests and for the Levites that waited.

Nehemiah 13:5 And he had prepared for him a great chamber, where aforetime they laid the meat offerings, the frankincense, and the vessels, and the tithes of the corn, the new wine, and the oil, which was commanded to be given to the Levites, and the singers, and the porters; and the offerings of the priests.

Nehemiah 13:12-13 Then brought all Judah the tithe of the corn and the new wine and the oil unto the treasuries. 13 And I made treasurers over the treasuries, Shelemiah the priest, and Zadok the scribe, and of the Levites, Pedaiah: and next to them was Hanan the son of Zaccur, the son of Mattaniah: for they were counted faithful, and their office was to distribute unto their brethren.

Psalms 50:14-15 Offer unto God thanksgiving; and pay thy vows unto the most High: 15 And call upon me in the day of trouble: I will deliver thee, and thou shalt glorify me.

Proverbs 3:9-10Honour the LORD with thy substance, and with the firstfruits of all thine increase: 10 So shall thy barns be filled with plenty, and thy presses shall burst out with new wine.

Proverbs 11:24-25 There is that scattereth, and yet increaseth; and there is that withholdeth more than is meet, but it tendeth to poverty. 25 The liberal soul shall be made fat: and he that watereth shall be watered also himself.

Proverbs 19:17 He that hath pity upon the poor lendeth unto the LORD; and that which he hath given will he pay him again.

Proverbs 22:9 He that hath a bountiful eye shall be blessed; for he giveth of his bread to the poor.

Ecclesiastes 5:4-5
When thou vowest a vow unto God, defer not to pay it; for he hath no pleasure in fools: pay that which thou hast vowed. 5 Better is it that thou shouldest not vow, than that thou shouldest vow and not pay.

Amos 4:4 Come to Bethel, and transgress; at Gilgal multiply transgression; and bring your sacrifices every morning, and your tithes after three years.

Malachi 3:10-11
Bring ye all the tithes into the storehouse, that there may be meat in mine house, and prove me now herewith, saith the LORD of hosts, if I will not open you the windows of heaven, and pour you out a blessing, that there shall not be room enough to receive it. 11 And I

will rebuke the devourer for your sakes, and he shall not destroy the fruits of your ground; neither shall your vine cast her fruit before the time in the field, saith the LORD of hosts.

Matthew 23:23
Woe unto you, scribes and Pharisees, hypocrites! for ye pay tithe of mint and anise and cummin, and have omitted the weightier matters of the law, judgment, mercy, and faith: these ought ye to have done, and not to leave the other undone.

Matthew 25:40 And the King shall answer and say unto them, Verily I say unto you, Inasmuch as ye have done it unto one of the least of these my brethren, ye have done it unto me.

But woe unto you, Pharisees! for ye tithe mint and rue and all manner of herbs, and pass over judgment and the love of God: these ought ye to have done, and not to leave the other undone. -Luke 11:42

Luke 6:38 Give, and it shall be given unto you; good measure, pressed down, and shaken together, and running over, shall men give into your bosom. For with the same measure that ye mete withal it shall be measured to you again.

Romans 12:13 Distributing to the necessity of saints; given to hospitality.

Leviticus 27:32 And concerning the tithe of the herd, or of the flock, even of whatsoever passeth under the rod, the tenth shall be holy unto the LORD.

Hebrews 7:1-9
For this Melchisedec, king of Salem, priest of the most high God, who met Abraham returning from the slaughter of the kings, and blessed him; 2 To whom also Abraham gave a tenth part of all; first being by interpretation King of righteousness, and after that also

King of Salem, which is, King of peace; 3 Without father, without mother, without descent, having neither beginning of days, nor end of life; but made like unto the Son of God; abideth a priest continually. :4 Now consider how great this man was, unto whom even the patriarch Abraham gave the tenth of the spoils. 5 And verily they that are of the sons of Levi, who receive the office of the priesthood, have a commandment to take tithes of the people according to the law, that is, of their brethren, though they come out of the loins of Abraham: 6 But he whose descent is not counted from them received tithes of Abraham, and blessed him that had the promises. 7 And without all contradiction the less is blessed of the better. 8 And here men that die receive tithes; but there he receiveth them, of whom it is witnessed that he liveth. 9 And as I may so say, Levi also, who receiveth tithes, payed tithes in Abraham.

Trust

Psalms 46:1-2
To the chief Musician for the sons of Korah, A Song upon Alamoth. God is our refuge and strength, a very present help in trouble. 2 Therefore will not we fear, though the earth be removed, and though the mountains be carried into the midst of the sea.

Psalms 84:12 For the LORD God is a sun and shield: the LORD will give grace and glory: no good thing will he withhold from them that walk uprightly. 12 O LORD of hosts, blessed is the man that trusteth in thee.

Psalms 37:3-5 Trust in the LORD, and do good; so shalt thou dwell in the land, and verily thou shalt be fed. 4 Delight thyself also in the LORD; and he shall give thee the desires of thine heart. 5 Commit thy way unto the LORD; trust also in him; and he shall bring it to pass.

Proverbs 3:5-6 Trust in the LORD with all thine heart; and lean not unto thine own understanding. 6 In all thy ways acknowledge him, and he shall direct thy paths. 7 Be not wise in thine.

Luke 12:32 Fear not, little flock; for it is your Father's good pleasure to give you the kingdom.

Matthew 6:31-32
Therefore take no thought, saying, what shall we eat? Or, what shall we drink? Or, Wherewithal shall we be clothed? 32 (For after all

these things do the Gentiles seek:) for your heavenly Father knoweth that ye have need of all these things.

1 Peter 5:7 Casting all your care upon him; for he careth for you.

Psalms 40:4 Blessed is that man that maketh the LORD his trust, and respecteth not the proud, nor such as turn aside to lies.

Psalms 125:1 A Song of degrees. They that trust in the LORD shall be as mount Zion, which cannot be removed, but abideth for ever.

Wisdom

James 1:5 If any of you lack wisdom, let him ask of God, that giveth to all men liberally, and upbraideth not; and it shall be given him.

Isaiah 2:3
And many people shall go and say, Come ye, and let us go up to the mountain of the LORD, to the house of the God of Jacob; and he will teach us of his ways, and we will walk in his paths: for out of Zion shall go forth the law, and the word of the LORD from Jerusalem.

Psalms32:8 I will instruct thee and teach thee in the way which thou shalt go: I will guide thee with mine eye.

Ecclesiastes 2:26
For God giveth to a man that is good in his sight wisdom, and knowledge, and joy: but to the sinner he giveth travail, to gather and to heap up, that he may give to him that is good before God. This also is vanity and vexation of spirit.

Psalms 16:7 I will bless the LORD, who hath given me counsel: my reins also instruct me in the night seasons.

Proverbs 2:5-7 Then shalt thou understand the fear of the LORD, and find the knowledge of God. 6 For the LORD giveth wisdom: out of his mouth cometh knowledge and understanding. 7 He layeth up sound wisdom for the righteous: he is a buckler to them that walk uprightly.

Psalms 51:6 Behold, thou desirest truth in the inward parts: and in the hidden part thou shalt make me to know wisdom.

1 John 5:20 And we know that the Son of God is come, and hath given us an understanding, that we may know him that is true, and we are in him that is true, even in his Son Jesus Christ. This is the true God, and eternal life.

2 Corinthians 4:6 For God, who commanded the light to shine out of darkness, hath shined in our hearts, to give the light of the knowledge of the glory of God in the face of Jesus Christ.

Proverbs 28:5 Evil men understand not judgment: but they that seek the LORD understand all things.

Word of God

Romans 1:16 For I am not ashamed of the gospel of Christ: for it is the power of God unto salvation to every one that believeth; to the Jew first, and also to the Greek.

Revelation 1:3 Blessed is he that readeth, and they that hear the words of this prophecy, and keep those things which are written therein: for the time is at hand.

2 Peter 1:19 Write the things which thou hast seen, and the things which are, and the things which shall be hereafter.

Hebrews 4:12 For the word of God is quick, and powerful, and sharper than any twoedged sword, piercing even to the dividing asunder of soul and spirit, and of the joints and marrow, and is a discerner of the thoughts and intents of the heart.

Psalms 119:130 The entrance of thy words giveth light; it giveth understanding unto the simple.

Proverbs 6:23 For the commandment is a lamp; and the law is light; and reproofs of instruction are the way of life.

Psalms 119:105 "… Thy word is a lamp unto my feet, and a light unto my path."

Johm5:39 Search the scriptures; for in them ye think ye have eternal life: and they are they which testify of me.

2 Timothy 3:15-16
And that from a child thou hast known the holy scriptures, which are able to make thee wise unto salvation through faith which is in Christ Jesus. 16 All scripture is given by inspiration of God, and is profitable for doctrine, for reproof, for correction, for instruction in righteousness.

Romans 10:17 So then faith cometh by hearing, and hearing by the word of God.

1 Peter 2:2 As newborn babes, desire the sincere milk of the word, that ye may grow thereby.

Deuteronomy 11:18 Therefore shall ye lay up these my words in your heart and in your soul, and bind them for a sign upon your hand, that they may be as frontlets between your eyes.

Joshua 1:8 This book of the law shall not depart out of thy mouth; but thou shalt meditate therein day and night, that thou mayest observe to do according to all that is written therein: for then thou shalt make thy way prosperous, and then thou shalt have good success.

James 1:21-25
Wherefore lay apart all filthiness and superfluity of naughtiness, and receive with meekness the engrafted word, which is able to save your souls. 22 But be ye doers of the word, and not hearers only, deceiving your own selves. 23 For if any be a hearer of the word, and not a doer, he is like unto a man beholding his natural face in a glass: 24 For he beholdeth himself, and goeth his way, and straightway forgetteth what manner of man he was. 25 But whoso looketh into the perfect law of liberty, and continueth therein, he

being not a forgetful hearer, but a doer of the work, this man shall be blessed in his deed.

1 Peter 1:23 Being born again, not of corruptible seed, but of incorruptible, by the word of God, which liveth and abideth for ever.

Acts 20:32 And now, brethren, I commend you to God, and to the word of his grace, which is able to build you up, and to give you an inheritance among all them which are sanctified.

Notes:

Notes:

Ovit G. Pursley Ministries™

Sow a Seed Today

*"...Pay thy vows unto the most high and call upon me in the day of trouble;" I will deliver thee...*Psalm: 50:14-15

Jesus is coming soon!

This is a good work, anointed of the Lord Jesus Christ.
Note: All Glory, Honor, Praise, and Thanksgiving is given unto God the Father, the Lord Jesus Christ, and the Holy Spirit for the knowledge and wisdom to compile all books by ***Ovit G. Pursley Ministries.***

Ovit G. Pursley Ministries Publishes Books, Bible studies for the Christian Market. The mission is to save, teach, strengthen, and establish believers in the faith. To provide a way for Ministers and Lay people to know Christ and make -Him known by publishing life-related materials that are Biblically rooted and: culturally reverent.

Ovit G. Pursley Personal Commission: "Go save, confirm, strengthen and establish believers in the Faith. Ministering both to the Spiritual and Physical needs of God's people, especially those who are starving for the sincere milk and meat of the Word. And lo I am with you always."

NOTICE: To Pastors, Ministers, Church Groups or Bible Study Groups; you may order in bulk (Large number of books for your congregation or study group). When doing so we recommend that you collect all money for each book and write a (one) check from the church or study group for the order. Thank You! Make your order TODAY!!!

Do something before it's too late!!!

Help me bless the body of Christ!
Sow a Seed Today!

Note: All Gifts, Love Offerings, Contributions, and Seed Sowing into this Ministry are highly appreciated to support this great work of God for the Body of Christ.

❑ I believe this is a work anointed of God! My Seed-Gift is:
❑ $50 ❑ $100 ❑ $200 ❑ $500 ❑ $1,000 ❑ $____________
❑ Enclosed is $________ toward *my* Vow of Faith.

Please make all checks and money orders payable in (U.S. FUNDS ONLY) to ***Ovit G. Pursley Ministries*** and send order with remittance to:

Ovit G. Pursley Ministries
P. O. Box 31574
Knoxville, TN 37930

"Give, and it shall be given unto you; good measure, pressed down, and shaken together, and running over, shall men give into your bosom. For with the same measure that ye mete withal it shall be measured to you again." Luke 6:38

Those wishing to contact Elder Ovit Pursley personally for ***Special Prayer, Contributions or to Sow Seed into this Ministry*** may write in care of the following address:

Ovit G. Pursley Ministries
P. O. Box 31574
Knoxville, TN 37930

***Feel free to copy this page to send with your seed offering!**
Name: ______________________________
Address: ______________________________
City: ______________ State __________ Zip: ____________
Email: ______________________________
Phone: (   ) ______________ Cell: (   ) ____________